DISASTER RESPONSE

IN

INDIA

Prakash Singh

William W. Mendel

Graham H. Turbiville, JR

A JOINT STUDY INITIATIVE BY
THE CENTER OF EXCELLENCE
IN DISASTER MANAGEMENT AND HUMANITARIAN
ASSISTANCE
AND
THE FOREIGN MILITARY STUDIES OFFICE
August 2000

DISCLAIMER

The views expressed in this report are those of the authors and do not necessarily represent the official policy or position of the Center of Excellence in Disaster Management and Humanitarian Assistance, Department of the Army, Department of Defense, or the U.S. Government.

The Center of Excellence in Disaster Management and Humanitarian Assistance was established in 1994 with the support of the U.S. Congress. Its mission is to create a world-class Center of Excellence to address a global mandate for the provision and facilitation of education, training and research in international disaster management and humanitarian assistance.

The Foreign Military Studies Office (FMSO) assesses regional security issues through open-source media and direct engagement with foreign academic and security specialists to advise leaders on issues of policy and planning critical to the U.S. Government and military community.

Please forward comments if any referencing this study to:

DIRECTOR
ATTN: ATIN-F (William W. Mendel)
FOREIGN MILITARY STUDIES OFFICE
101 MEADE AVE
FORT LEAVENWORTH KS 66027-1351

This edition published by Books Express Publishing
Copyright © Books Express, 2011
ISBN 978-1-1780391-42-7
To purchase copies please contact info@books-express.com

Map
of
INDIA

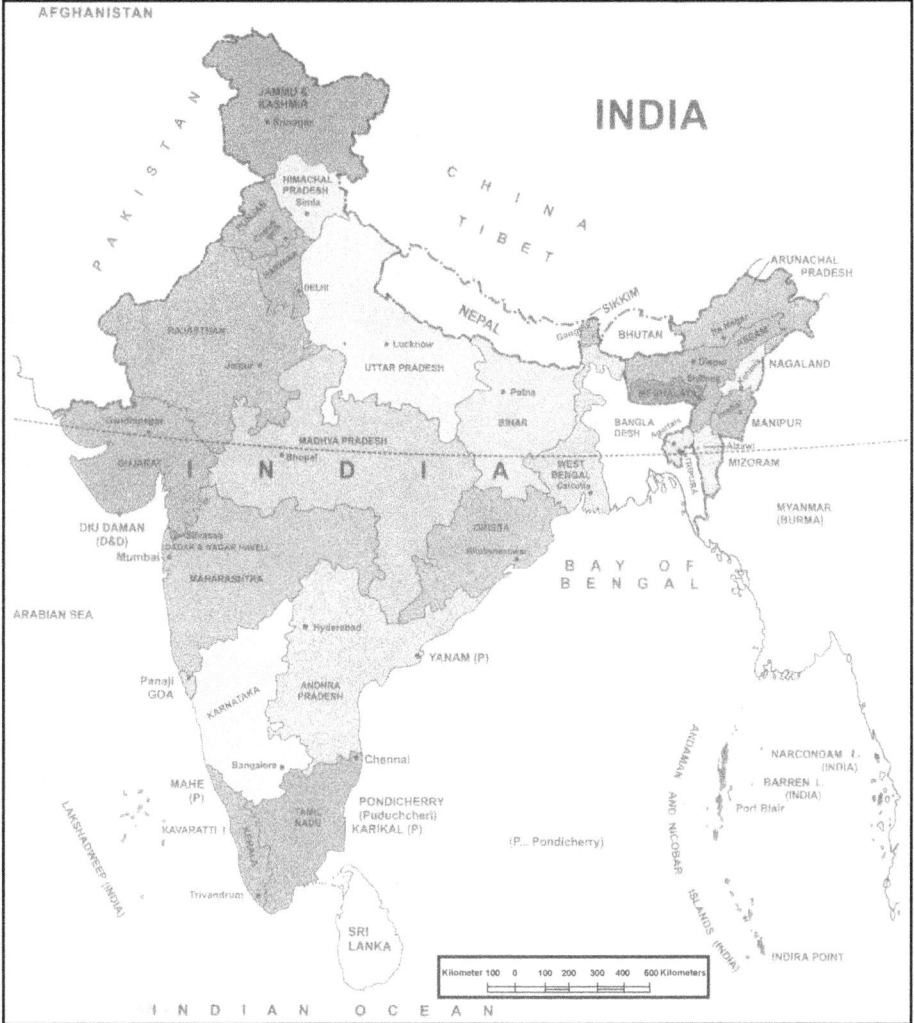

Figure i. Map of India. Source: Government of India.

India - States and Union Territories

States/UTs	Capital	Area	Population (1991 Census)	Principal Languages
States				
Andhra Pradesh (AP)	Hyderabad	275,068	66,508,008	Telugu and Urdu
Arunachal Pradesh	Itanagar	83,743	864,558	Monpa, Miji, Aka, Nishing, etc.
Assam	Dispur	78,438	2,414,322	Assamese
Bihar	Patna	173,877	86,374,465	Hindi
Goa	Panaji	3,702	1,169,793	Konkani, Marathi
Gujarat	Gandhinagar	196,024	41,309,582	Gujarati
Haryana	Chandigarh	44,212	16,463,648	Hindi
Himachal Pradesh (HP)	Shimla	55,673	5,170,877	Hindi, Pahari
Jammu and Kashmir (J&K)	Srinagar	222,236	7,718,700	Urdu, Kashmiri, Dogri, Ladakhi
Karnataka	Bangalore	191,791	44,977,201	Kannada
Kerala	Thiruvanantha--puram	38,863	29,098,518	Malayalam
Madhya Pradesh (MP)	Bhopal	443,446	66,181,000	Hindi
Maharashtra	Mumbai	307,713	78,937,187	Marathi
Manipur	Imphal	22,327	1,837,149	Manipuri
Meghalaya	Shillong	22,429	1,774,778	Khasi, Garo, English
Mizoram	Aizawl	21,081	689,756	Mizo, English
Nagaland	Kohima	16,579	1,209,546	Angami, Sema, Konyak, etc.
Orissa	Bhubaneswar	155,707	31,659,736	Oriya
Punjab	Chandigarh	50,362	20,281,969	Punjabi
Rajasthan	Jaipur	342,239	44,005,990	Hindi, Rajasthani
Sikkim	Gangtok	7,096	406,457	Lepcha, Bhutia, Nepali, Limbu
Tamilnadu	Chennai	130,058	55,858,946	Tamil
Tripura	Agartala	10,492	2,757,205	Bengali,Kok Borak
Uttar Pradesh (UP)	Lucknow	294,411	139,112,287	Hindi, Urdu
West Bengal (WB)	Calcutta	88,752	67,982,732	Bengali
Union Territories				
Andaman and Nicobar Islands	Port Blair	8,249	280,661	Hindi, Nicobarese, Malayalam, Tamil, Telugu
Chandigarh	Chandigarh	114	642,015	Punjabi, Hindi
Dadra and Nagar Haveli	Silvassa	491	138,477	Gujarati, Hindi
Daman and Diu	Daman	112	101,586	Gujarati
Delhi	Delhi	1,483	9,420,644	Hindi, Punjabi
Lakshadweep	Kavaratti	32	5,1707	Malayalam
Pondicherrry	Pondicherry	492	807,785	Tamil, Telugu, English, French

Figure ii. India-States and Union Territories.

Table of Contents

EXECUTIVE SUMMARY 1

   I. INDIA'S DISASTER MANAGEMENT 13
       Addressing the Basics 13
       India's Situation 15
       Managing Disasters 18

  II. HISTORICAL PERSPECTIVE 23
       Floods 23
       Droughts and Famines...27
       Earthquakes 31
       Cyclones 35
       Other Disasters 39

 III. PLANNING FACTORS: Land, People,
       and Infrastructure..43
       The Subcontinent: Geography and Geology 43
       Population..47
       Infrastructure 50

 IV. SERVICES 71
       Medical and Public Health 71
       Fire Fighting...73
       Civil Defense..73
       Home Guards..74
       Police 75
       Paramilitary Forces...77
       Defense Forces 78
       Role of the Armed Forces in Disaster Relief 82

  V. NATIONAL, STATE AND LOCAL LEVELS OF
       GOVERNMENT 89
       National Level...90
       State Level..96
       District Level..99
       Financial Arrangements 100

VI.   NGOs, INTERNATIONAL ORGANIZATIONS,
AND COMMUNITY EFFORTS 105
      NGO Roles 105
      NGOs Working in India 107
      United Nations' Role 112
      Donor Countries 113
      Self-reliance and Sovereignty 113
      Timely, Effective Support 114

VII. EXAMPLES OF DISASTER RESPONSE 119
      Flood 120
      Drought 125
      Earthquake 127
      Cyclone 129
      Landslide 132
      Technological Disaster: Bhopal 134

VIII. INDIA'S DISASTER MANAGEMENT
EVIRONMENT 149
      Falling Short 150
      Moving Ahead 152
      Assessing the Environment 153
      The Nuclear Specter and Natural Disasters 156

      BIBLIOGRAPHY 161

      ANNEX – NGOs in INDIA 169

      INDEX 179

List of Figures

    i. Map of India..iii

   ii. India-States and Union Territories...v

  I-1. Annual Average Number of People Killed or Affected
       by Region and Period...16

  I-2. India's Disaster Vulnerability 17

  II-1. Earthquake Examples...32

  II-2. Examples of Cyclone Disasters...36

 III-1. Section of Southwest Asia 44

 III-2. Average Annual Temperature and Rainfall 46

 III-3. Population of Selected Countries...47

 III-4. Population Growth of India, Projected to 2016 49

 III-5. National Railroad & Highway System...................................53

 III-6. Accidental Deaths and Suicides in India, 1996.....................55

 IV-1. State Police Organization..75

 IV-2. Central Paramilitary Forces..77

 IV-3. Army Organization..80

 IV-4. Army Areas 81

  V-1. Scarcity Relief Division 92

  V-2. Interaction Among Ministries and Departments 93

  V-3. State Disaster Management, Levels of Administration..........96

VII-1. Northern Flood Areas, 1988..120

VII-2. Eastern Flood Areas, 1998 123

VII-3. Gujarat Cyclone, 1998 130

VII-4. Landslide Disaster, 1998..133

VII-5. Bhopal and Union Carbide Plant..135

Foreword

The Center of Excellence in Disaster Management and Humanitarian Assistance is pleased to have sponsored the research that went into the completion of this report, a substantive reference text that shall be useful to disaster management and planning professionals worldwide for many years to come. Its four primary partners, U.S. Pacific Command, Tripler Army Medical Center, the University of Hawaii and the Centers for Disease Control and Prevention act collectively to support a body of operational research. *Disaster Response in India* represents the first product of these efforts.

The Center of Excellence, a unique and forward-thinking partnership, acts as a facilitator among the many organizations which are critical players in the delivery of disaster management, relief and recovery. Its research mission cuts across organizational boundaries and thus the Center is able to identify proposals of universal benefit. Focusing through a collaborative lens allows the Center to work with more appropriate, multi-pronged approaches leveraged across civilian, military and private partnerships. The commitment to support operational research in a variety of fields and disciplines - from public and mental health issues in refugee populations to re-establishing functioning infrastructure in devastated communities - evolved from the core purposes of the Center, which is to bring together the best individuals and organizations who are dedicated to improving the world's ability to respond to natural and complex humanitarian events.

The authors' work herein, the culmination of many hours of intensive labor, contributes to an appreciation of foreign disaster management processes, encourages international cooperation, and supports disaster management institutions and professionals in all countries and regions. To conduct and publish findings as these is of benefit to all peoples. In our shrinking, interdependent world, the drop of even a small stone in one place leads to ripples felt in the most remote corners of the world.

It is our hope that this document will see widespread distribution, and through extensive use that it be passed along to colleagues as a tome on the topic.

Fredrick M. Burkle, Jr., MD, MPH
Director,
Center of Excellence in
Disaster Management and Humanitarian Assistance

Acknowledgements

The authors appreciate the support provided by these disaster management officials and humanitarians who are working in India to mitigate potential disaster situations and who lend direct needed assistance whenever a crisis unfolds: Mr. O. P. Tandon, IPS (retired); Mr. Bhagat Singh, IAS, Additional Secretary, Ministry of Agriculture; Peter McAllister, Assistant Country Director and Harry S. Sethi, Director of Special Projects, CARE-India; Santosh Clare, Material Aid Officer, Churches Auxiliary for Social Action (CASA); Peter Delahaye, Deputy Director (Operations) and Mr. S.S. Alam, Procurement Officer, United Nations Children's Fund (UNICEF); Dr. Unnikrishnan P. V., OXFAM Fellow for Emergencies; Dr. Heather W. Goldman, the Director of the Office of Social Development and Mission Disaster Relief Officer, USAID, U.S. Mission to India; Dr. R. B. Sharma, Director, Dr. Rakesh Dubey, Joint Director and Mr. Lokendra Thakkar, Manager for Awareness, Documentation and Information, Disaster Management Institute (DMI), Bhopal; Satinath Sarangi, Director, Bhopal Peoples Health and Documentation Clinic, Sambhavna Trust, Bhopal; Colonel Mark Pernell, Defense Attache, U.S. Embassy, New Delhi; Mr. M. C. Gupta, Director of Indian Institute of Public Administration and Coordinator, National Center for Disaster Management (NCDM); Dr. J. N. Upadhyay, Dr. Vinod K. Sharma, and Dr. Girish K. Misra of the NCDM, New Delhi. They also appreciate the excellent work of Mr. Arvind Kandpal of India and Mr. Edward J. Carr, visual information specialist of Fort Leavenworth, Kansas who prepared the manuscript and figures for publication. Finally, we are grateful for the support provided by Gary J. Rhyne, Centers for Disease Control and Prevention (CDC) public health advisor to the Center of Excellence in Disaster Management and Humanitarian Assistance (COE) and the vision and encouragement of Dr. Frederick "Skip" Burkle, Director, COE.

Executive Summary

Elephants on the
Rajpath Defending
Rashtrapati Bhavan
(President's Palace)

India is prone to natural and man-made disasters. The number has been increasing every year because of the mixture of various factors such as adverse weather, population growth, urbanization, and industrialization. How the Republic of India organizes for managing significant natural and man-made disasters, its capacity for effective response, and its ability to achieve unity of effort among governmental and non-governmental organizations are the elements of analysis here. This is of interest because India is an emerging world power; it is currently the second largest country in the world in population, and by 2050 it will have surpassed China as the largest.

The number of Indians affected by disaster events shows a steady upward trend. Disasters have been taking a heavy toll of human and animal lives. Floods have proven to be the most devastating type of natural disaster in India, causing the maximum number of deaths and damage to property (cyclones have taken a heavy toll of lives and caused widespread devastation). At the same time, droughts affect a large segment of population, resulting in loss of employment and migration to other regions. Earthquakes have caused a comparatively lower amount of damage, but landslides are likely to increase in frequency in the coming years because of deforestation and over development on hillsides. Conurbation and industrialization have combined to create a dangerous synergy that now presents a significant hazard to India's people.

In responding to these kinds of hazards, India's disaster management officials and professional humanitarians conduct disaster planning and response generally within a paradigm of three phases: *Pre-disaster; Emergency* (or Disaster Impact); *Post Disaster* (or Recovery). There is a strong emphasis in government policy and planning to encourage mitigation, i.e., actions taken prior to the occurrence of a disaster, including preparedness and long-term risk reduction measures.

1

To encourage effective training, coordination and planning for disaster response, the Government of India established in 1995 a National Center for Disaster Management; and in 1998, India's Minister for Agriculture announced the formation of a National Commission on Disaster Management. These will facilitate the evolution of a National Disaster Management Plan. The Plan is now under development and is expected to be completed in 2001.

RESPONSE SYSTEM

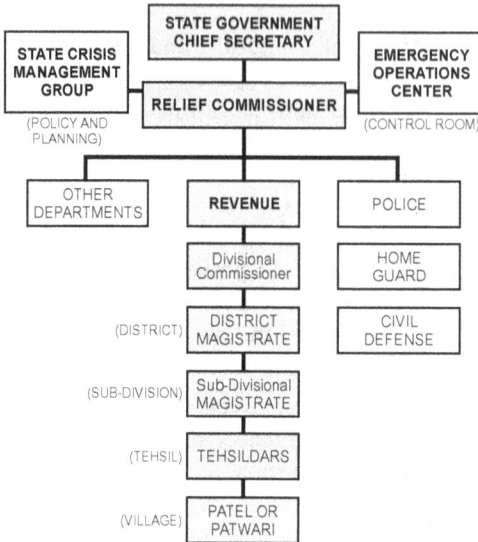

TYPICAL ORGANIZATION FOR STATE EMERGENCY

Under India's federal system, the states have responsibility for disaster response. When the disasters is severe or spread over several states, the Central Government supplements the efforts of state governments by providing financial and material assistance.

Government policy response to a natural calamity is provided by the Prime Minister, Cabinet Committees and the Agriculture Minister. The objectives of policy response are to address the sufferings of the people affected by the natural calamity. A policy response often leads to visits to the calamity affected areas by President, Prime Minister and other dignitaries; setting up machinery for implementing, reviewing and monitoring the relief measures; and activating the administrative response process for assistance in relief measures.

The state governments in India are autonomous in organizing relief operations in the event of natural disaster and also for purposes of long term preparedness and rehabilitation measures. The states deal with natural disasters through their Revenue Departments or Relief Organizations.

The states also have a State Crisis Management Group (SCMG) which functions under the chairmanship of Chief Secretary and/or Relief Commissioner. The Group comprises senior officers from the departments of revenue and relief, home, civil supplies, power, irrigation, water supply, local self government (*panchayat*), agriculture, forests, rural development, health, planning, public works and finance. States develop the contingency plans for disaster response and long-term strategies for mitigation.

The state response plan identifies the functional areas such as relief, communications, information, transport, health services, etc. and proposes assignments to the various departments. The plan also lays down preparedness checklists, operating procedures and reporting formats. The state mitigation strategy argues for better land use management, building codes, traffic standards, health standards, and so on. These objectives are to be secured through disaster legislation, mitigation regulation, and incentives for mitigation.

The State Relief Commissioner establishes an Emergency Operations Center (Control Room) as soon as disaster situation develops. The Center collects and disseminates the latest information on forecasting and warning of disaster, and functions as the focal point for coordinating disaster relief efforts with the other concerned departments.

THE FIRST RESPONDERS

Every state is divided into a number of districts. The head of the district administration is known as the District Magistrate or Deputy Commissioner. (In some states, he is better known as the Collector). The District Magistrate is in charge of all the relief measures at the district level. The State government routes its instructions through him, and the District Magistrate ensures that the total efforts of the district are geared in a coordinated manner to providing disaster relief to the people. Sometimes, in emergency situations, the District Magistrate's powers are enhanced with a view to ensuring complete unison in the efforts of all the concerned departments.

A district is further sub-divided into sub-divisions and tehsils. The head of the sub-division is called a Sub-Divisional Officer or Deputy Collector while the tehsil is headed by an officer called the Tehsildar. The lowest unit of administration is the village whose revenue matters are attended to by a functionary known as Patel or Patwari. These lower tiers of administration provide the first responders that do the work, and they are a critically important source of leadership during disaster events.

When disaster strikes, the District Magistrate activates his contingency plan with the help of Control Room staff who monitor rescue and relief efforts. Also assisting is the District Relief Committee which includes local representatives of the people, members of the legislative assembly and the parliament. Through these mechanisms, the District Magistrate coordinates with central government authorities and defense forces, and he synchronizes the voluntary efforts of NGOs with the efforts of the district administration.

THE NGOS

India has a strong tradition of voluntary organizations responding to any calamity or disaster overwhelming the people. The voluntary organizations offer immediately available communications within the disaster affected community, technical services, manpower, and financial support. Services provided by the NGOs include awareness and information campaigns, training for local volunteers, immediate rescue and first aid, psychological aid, food, water, medicine, other materials, sanitation and hygiene, damage assessment, reconstruction and financial aid.

The 1998 cyclone in Gujarat provides some idea of the scope of NGO emergency assistance during a disaster event in India:

- *CARE-India:* food for two months and 350 tents worth Rs. 700,000;

- *CARITAS:* housing reconstruction;

- *Catholic Relief Service:* $10,000 for shelter and drinking water, and 161 tonnes of food supplies;

- *The Discipleship Center:* plastic sheets, utensils, bed sheets, *sarees, dhotis,* and children's clothing;

- *OXFAM:* food grains, plastic sheets, clothing;

- *World Vision:* roof tiles, wood materials for home reconstruction.

India prefers not to request disaster assistance in any formal way from donor nations or international organizations. Its stated policy is that India will rely on its own resources to resolve disaster situations. But it is difficult to imagine disaster relief operations without the contributions of the international and India-based NGOs. To avoid being at cross purposes with Indian policy, international organizations and donor nations usually provide disaster assistance resources to local level governments and grass-roots organizations via on-site NGOs.

DISASTER RESPONSE AND SYSTEM PERFORMANCE

Disaster events in recent years have placed great demands on India's disaster management system, and the year 1998 was a particularly bad one for the country. Floods affected several states. A cyclone of severe intensity devastated Gujarat. Landslides took a heavy toll of human lives in the hill regions of Uttar Pradesh. The Orissa cyclone of 1999 was the greatest natural disaster the country has faced in the 20th century. These hazards illustrate the magnitude of the challenge.

Floods

There were unprecedented rains in Punjab, Haryana, Himachal Pradesh and Jammu & Kashmir in September 1988. In Kapurthala district, the water from Beas river submerged about 150 villages under 8 to 12 feet of water. In Jalandhar, fifty per cent of the standing crops were destroyed. In Ropar, thousands of people were trapped in flood waters and had to spend several nights on the rooftops of their houses. Gurdaspur town had two to four feet of water.

The Government of India formed a Crisis Management Group under the chairmanship of the Relief Commissioner. The Armed Forces helped to evacuate people, and provided air, land and water transportation. A voluntary body known as Flood Relief Society was formed with Justice Ajit Singh Bains, a retired judge of the Punjab and Haryana High Court, as Chairman to provide relief to the flood affected people of Punjab. The Society made Sikh and Hindu temples the focal points for collecting relief material.

In Himachal Pradesh, Kinnaur, Una, Chamba, Kulu and Shimla were badly affected. More than a dozen bridges in different parts of the State collapsed, and about two thousand persons were marooned in the Pong dam area. Una was completely cut off. People living in Chamba along the Ravi river had to be shifted to safer places.

The Border Security Forces personnel were marooned at their outposts. Thein dam was threatened. The Grand Trunk Road between Beas, Rayya and Khalichain was submerged under three to four feet of water.

Over 405 thousand cubic feet per second (cusecs) of water was flowing in river Sutlej on September 24 against its capacity of 305 thousand cusecs. There was panic about the safety of the Bhakra Dam. The reservoir attained the highest ever level of 1687.47 ft., which was above the maximum storage level designed for the dam. The Bhakra Beas Management Board (BBMB) released the extra water without bothering about the capacity of the reservoirs below. The BBMB did not warn the district authorities or the people before releasing the water. People in areas downstream were caught unawares–aggravating the magnitude of the disaster. There was loss of life and property on a massive scale. In northern areas of India, catchment areas have deteriorated due to increasing deforestation and urbanization leading to the reservoirs getting silted, their storage capacity reduced, and life span cut short.

The 1998 floods also affected large areas of northern and eastern states with Upper Assam being the worst affected. Nearly 5,000 villages were submerged, and a total of 3.6 million people were affected by the fury of the Brahmaputra river. Majuli, the largest river island in the world, was completely submerged and over 100,000 people living on the island had to be evacuated.

In West Bengal, more than half the total population of Malda were rendered homeless–1.5 million people. Large areas of Murshidabad were inundated by the Bhagirathi river. Army and the Border Security Force personnel assisted the State administration in the rescue and relief operations. The Navy also sent boats and a team of 50 people including doctors to Malda.

In Bihar, a total of nearly 12 million people in over 7,200 villages in 28 districts in north and central Bihar were affected. Army personnel assisted in relief works in Katihar and Darbhanga districts.

There were floods in Uttar Pradesh, Madhya Pradesh, Orissa, Arunachal Pradesh and Meghalaya also. The severity of flooding in these states was comparatively less in the strategic sense, but no less serious to the victims.

Cyclones in Gujarat and Orissa

Gujarat state was lashed by a severe cyclonic storm on June 9, 1998. About 1,250 people were killed while over one thousand were reported missing. There was devastation on a large scale in the districts of Kutch, Jamnagar, Rajkot, Porbandar, Junagadh, Amreli, Bhavnagar, Banaskantha, Surat, Bharuch, Valsad and Navsari. Nearly 66 hectares of agricultural land was eroded and thousands of trees were uprooted.

The gateway along the Gulf of Kutch became a graveyard of vessels with 40 ships having run aground and five of them actually sinking.

The Gujarat government reacted with a "caterpillar-like pace," according to *India Today* magazine. In the State Assembly, the Congress members, during discussions on the tragedy, harped on the point that a majority of lives lost on June 9, 1998 along the Saurashtra-Kutch coastline could have been saved had the State Government implemented a sound disaster management plan. The Union Home Minister conceded that the cyclone forecast of the Meteorological Department had gone awry as there was no mention in its forecast that Kutch district, which was worst affected, would be hit. There was also lack of communication between the Kandla Port Trust Authorities and the district administration.

It also came to light that the Kandla Port Trust had been repeatedly warned about the consequences of tampering with coastal ecosystems and building too many new projects in the Kandla Port area. Political considerations had led to project after project being cleared. The Government of Gujarat had even altered the Coastal Management Plan to facilitate projects in the Coastal Regulation Zone.

In recent years, construction of chemical facilities, petroleum complexes, cement factories, ports and jetties had stripped the coastal natural barriers formed by coral outcrops, sand banks, mangrove plants and dunes. Nothing remained to impede the 200 km/h cyclonic winds and four-meter tidal waves—a large number of innocents died.

In response, the Government of India decided to give assistance to the maritime states in the Ninth Plan for the protection of critical reaches of coastal areas. Under this scheme, the coastal areas would be protected by constructing sea walls. The Coastal Protection and Development Advisory Committee has prepared a comprehensive National Coastal Protection Project estimated to cost Rs. 16 billion.

The cyclone which lashed Orissa on October 29, 1999 has been described by Sitakant Mahapatra as "perhaps the greatest tragedy Orissa has faced since the Kalinga war that converted... Ashoka to Buddhism." The death toll was over 10,000 and the total loss of property has been estimated at Rs. 10 billion.

Landslides

On August 18, 1998, a massive landslide wiped out the entire Malpa village in the Pithoragarh district of Uttar Pradesh, killing about 210 people. Earlier, 76 people were killed in devastating landslides in the

Ukhimath block of Rudraprayag district on August 12. There were landslides in the Ukhimath area again on August 19, killing 26 people. A total of nearly 400 people are estimated to have been killed and 12 villages were wiped out in a series of landslides spread over a period of ten days in the hill regions of Uttar Pradesh.

A team of 200 personnel from the Army, Indo-Tibetan Border Police, Pradeshik Armed Constabulary and Border Security Force was rushed to Malpa to carry out the relief operations. The State Government announced an ex gratia of Rs. one hundred thousand each to the next of kin of those killed in the tragedy, Rs. 50,000.00 each to the injured, and Rs. 25,000.00 for the reconstruction of damaged houses.

The community response was spontaneous. A correspondent who toured the region commented that the Ukhimath community set a stellar example in altruism. Every family fed at least one person affected by the landslides. "We take it that every family has one more member to look after," as a student of the Garhwal University said. The *Yuvak Mangal Dal* and the *Mahila Mangal Dal*, voluntary associations of youth and women in the region, did yeoman's service in rushing to the unsafe areas with succor. The Himalayan Environment Studies and Conservation Organization, an NGO, sent medicines and relief materials.

In spite of recurring landslides in the region, adequate attention has not been paid to planning and preventative measures. The cumulative effects of deforestation, erosion, water-logging, salinity and nutrient depletion all over the country have led to a loss of approximately Rs.232 billion.

Technological Disaster–Long-term Effects Remain

The Bhopal gas tragedy, which took place on December 3, 1984, was the worst technological disaster of the country. It was the result of faulty design, poor maintenance and unsatisfactory plant operation. Union Carbide, a U.S.-based multinational company, had a plant manufacturing Sevin and other pesticides at Bhopal. On the night of December 2, methyl isocyanate (MIC) gas escaped into Bhopal's night air. It is estimated that as as many as 18,000 human deaths resulted from the incident, and large numbers of livestock perished.

Today, some 15 years after the event, relatively few people have been properly compensated for their losses, and there are perhaps as many as 125,000 people who are in an acute state of ill health as a result of a whole range of diseases like breathlessness, eye problems,

8

neurological disorders, menstrual and other reproductive abnormalities, anxiety, depression and obstructive pulmonary disease.

The Bhopal experience has provided a number of lessons, such as the need to regulate the growth of industries producing hazardous products. The most important of these is suggested by Dr. R. B. Sharma, Director of the Disaster Management Institute in Bhopal:

> *The basic point of disaster management recovery is the human dimension. We are too concerned with the material. There is little attention to what happens after the disaster.*

The cyclones, earthquakes, floods, and landslides of 1998 and 1999, as well as the lingering effects of the Bhopal tragedy, suggest the grand dimensions of India's disaster management challenge. It also suggests the capabilities and capacities for disaster management in India today.

THE FUTURE FOR INDIA'S DISASTER MANAGEMENT

The overall trend is towards more disaster-related deaths and losses. Some reasons for this are:

- Continuing population growth which will overload the available infrastructure and services, even without the advent of disasters;

- Increasing pressure on a land that will have to feed the world's most populous nation but, year after year, is vulnerable to the vagaries of weather;

Bhopal: The Union Carbide Plant as it Appears Today.

- Uneven economic growth that may result in a better life for some sectors while leaving others destitute and unable to ward off hazards;

- Interdependence of countries and regions whereby hazards in one region impact directly on others, such as low-land flooding caused by denudation of upland forests, or a nuclear accident in one region which casts fallout on another.

Experience shows that in the event of a disaster, the government response is generally tardy. Critics suggest that this is because the bureaucracy, which was once considered the "steel frame" of administration, has over the years become inefficient and corrupt. Millions are spent on flood protection schemes and drought relief measures, but only a fraction really shows. Analyzing disaster management in India, *Times of India* commentator Rajiv Desai recently wrote:

> *Lives are lost, families ruined and property is destroyed. The only survivors are those who govern: politicians, bureaucrats and their retinue. ...no one is held accountable for public safety. Thus, the very minimum requirement of governance is waived. Never mind disaster management, the government itself is the disaster.*

The Government of India has the requisite structure to cope with disasters. There are detailed orders and manuals on related subjects, particularly at the state level. However, the Central Government has yet to publish a national emergency management plan and lacks the formal and official framework for strategic guidance and doctrinal development. Nevertheless, the confluence of effort by professionals associated with organizations such as the National Center for Disaster Management, Disaster Management Institute, Indira Gandhi National Open University, and so on, has developed a body of knowledge relevant to India's situation.

The universal themes which have evolved from this effort suggest the following doctrinal imperatives for future initiatives:

- A strong focus on disaster prevention and mitigation;
- Long-term measures to fight earthquake–economic and technical effort;
- Control of economic development to reduce the impact on the land and resulting changes to the flow of water run-off;
- Setaside funding by the states for disaster emergencies, augmented by Central Government grants;
- The need for networking among disaster management organizations, government agencies, and non-government volunteer organizations;

- An emphasis on training and publishing the professional body of knowledge;

- Emphasis on the human dimension of disasters, particularly the social, medical, and psychological aspects of long-term recovery.

Given India's constitutional guidelines of state responsibility for disaster management, a ponderous bureaucracy, an historical preference for devolving responsibility to regional levels of government, it seems likely that India's forthcoming National Disaster Management Plan will provide generalized policy constructs. The locus of disaster prevention and relief will remain with state governments, with the primary burden carried by the District Magistrate.

Under siege by the current onslaught of cyclones, floods, earthquakes, and landslides, nuclear weapons bring an added dimension to India's disaster management challenge. The confrontation between India and Pakistan over the Kashmir problem poses a proximate threat to peace and stability in the sub-continent. The acquisition of nuclear capability by both India and Pakistan has added a new and unwanted component to disaster prevention and assistance.

As some Indian disaster specialists suggest, there remains some comfort in what seems to be India's almost unlimited capacity to absorb shocks. There have been waves of invasion from across the north-west frontier through the centuries, but the spirit of India was never vanquished. India always reasserted itself, and with this spirit of certitude India will approach the coming challenges of disaster response in the new millennium.

I. India's Disaster Management

Himself creates. Himself preserves. Himself destroys.[1]

Tirumantiram

A mong the challenges facing Pacific Rim countries today is the problem of preparing for and managing responses to natural and man-made disasters. For many, such hazards can represent a direct threat to economic and political stability, necessary precursors for healthy democracies. The capacity of countries for assisting themselves is of keen interest to private and government humanitarians and disaster management professionals. This can be an indicator of the capability of the state to support emergency assistance and recovery operations in neighboring countries as well.

How the Republic of India organizes for managing significant natural and man-made disasters, its capacity for effective response, and its ability to achieve unity of effort among governmental and non-governmental organizations are the central elements of analysis here. India is an emerging world power; it is currently the second most populous country in the world, and by 2050 it will have surpassed China in population.[2]

India's ability to help itself and help others is important to the professionals who do the planning and operations for emergency support in times of great need. Thus, for the Honolulu-based Center Of Excellence in Disaster Management and Humanitarian Assistance, gaining an understanding of India's disaster management processes, as well as lessons learned from recent disasters, is important for its international mandate to facilitate education, training, and research.[3] This study represents a COE initiative to contribute toward disaster assistance knowledge through the Indian experience.

ADDRESSING THE BASICS

The World Health Organization assesses disaster as an occurrence that causes damage, economic destruction, loss of human life and deterioration in health and the health services on a scale sufficient to warrant an extraordinary response from outside the affected community or area. Another definition of disaster states that it is "an occurrence arising with little or no warning, which causes or threatens serious disruption of life, and perhaps death or injury to large numbers of people, and requires therefore a mobilization of effort in excess of that normally provided by the statutory emergency services."[4] It is seen also as an event "that produces the conditions whereby the continuity of the structure and processes of social units become problematic..." as observed in India during repeated cyclones and flooding.[5]

The Indian *Encyclopaedia of Disaster Management,* edited by P. C. Sinha, describes disasters using the typology of natural, man-made, or a hybrid of the two.

—*Natural Disasters* include floods, earthquake, volcanic eruption, hurricane, tornado, and avalanche;

—*Man-made disasters* (or those with anthropogenic origin) are exemplified by some of the terrible accidents that have resulted from man's interaction with the artificial environment he has created, such as the nuclear accident at Chernobyl and the methyl isocyanate (MIC) gas tragedy at Bhopal;

—*Hybrid Disasters* can arise from a combination of anthropogenic and natural events like the destruction of rain forests (and resulting increased severity of flooding or mudslides) or deaths due to heat waves and pollution in the major conurbations around the world.[6]

Sinha makes the point that although it is difficult to identify a clear pattern of disaster events, we should be able to discern general patterns of man-made development and settlement that are attendant to severe disasters. For some 17 categories of disaster, he suggests a high degree of human involvement illustrated here:[7]

Disaster Type	Natural	Man-Made	Hybrid
Avalanche/Rockfall	yes	No	yes
Air Transport	no	yes	yes
Road Transport	no	yes	yes
Marine Transport	no	yes	yes
Rail Transport	no	yes	yes
Climatic	yes	no	yes
Drought	yes	yes	yes
Famine	yes	yes	yes
Epidemic	yes	no	yes
Plague	yes	yes	yes
Earthquake	yes	no	no

Disaster Type	Natural	Man-Made	Hybrid
Fire	yes	yes	yes
Explosion	no	yes	yes
Flooding	yes	no	yes
Mining	no	yes	yes
Volcanic Activity	yes	no	yes

In addition, we can be faced with *Compound Disasters* when one type of hazard triggers a disaster which, in turn, triggers another hazard and subsequent disaster. A drought may lead to a famine which may result in a civil conflict leading to mass displacement of people. *Complex Disasters* are emergencies in which the contributory causes and the assistance to the affected people are circumscribed by political considerations. The disaster becomes complex because the collapse or breakdown of political authority makes assistance highly problematic. A way out of the impasse is found through an agreement between the parties involved in the conflict with humanitarian considerations prevailing over all the other considerations. The situation in Sarajevo, where conflicts among Bosnian Muslims and Serbs enjoined U.N. participation, falls into this category.

Disaster causes and factors have been categorized in other ways too. The nature of *Sudden Onset Hazards* can be geological (earthquake, Tsunami, volcanic eruption, landslide) and climatic (tropical cyclone, flood). *Slow Onset Hazards* are typically environmental in nature (pollution, deforestation, desertification, and pest infestation). *Industrial and Technological Hazards* (systems failure and accidents, explosions and fires, nuclear mishap) and *War and Civil Strife* (armed aggression, terrorism, and insurgency) are also prominent factors.

Disasters of different kinds have taken a very heavy toll of human lives all over the world. During the twenty-five year period (1972-1996), according to the *World Disasters Report, 1998* , the annual average number of people killed (by region and by period, 1972 to 1996) have been as shown in Figure I-1 below.[8]

INDIA'S SITUATION

India is prone to natural disasters, and the number has been increasing every year due to the combined effects of adverse weather, population growth, urbanization, and industralization. As a result, the

	Africa	America	Asia	Europe	Oceania	TOTAL
1973 to 1977	84,413	8,519	68,454	2,318	107	163,811
1978 to 1982	1,436	3,172	16,529	1,406	35	22,579
1983 to 1987	115,269	10,853	17,073	2,302	189	145,686
1988 to 1992	12,272	5,248	63,435	2,352	138	83,445
1993 to 1997	7,919	3,065	19,078	1,996	149	32,206
1973 to 1997	44,262	6,171	36,914	2,075	124	89,546

Figure I-1, Annual Average Number of People Killed by Region and Period. Source: *World Disasters Report 1999.* Note: Africa's high figures resulted from 1972-75 drought in the Horn (Sudan Ethiopia, Djibouti, Somalia) and the Sahel (Mali, Niger); and 1982-86 drought in the Sahel (Sudan, Ethiopia).

number of people affected also shows a steady of upward trend. These disasters have been taking a heavy toll of human and animal lives and disrupting the life-supporting systems, which are basically at nature's mercy. Disaster management professionals are quick to identify these features:

–Floods are the most devastating type of natural disaster in India, causing the maximum number of deaths and damage to property (and cyclones are next only to that of floods);

—Droughts affect a large segment of population, resulting in loss of employment and migration, but the casualties are not so heavy;

—Earthquakes have shown a comparatively lower capacity to cause damages;

—Landslides are likely to increase in frequency in the coming years because of deforestation in the catchment areas and unplanned constructions in the hills.

–Conurbation and industrialization can combine to effect a dangerous synergy resulting in a significant hazard to populations.

A 1998 study by the Maharashtra State Government concerning *Risk Assessment and Vulnerability Analysis* for the Indian Subcontinent focused on trends and issues concerning number of lives lost, people affected (compared to total regional population), and significant damage (damage of one percent or more of GNP). It confirms that floods are the most problematic hazards for the region (involving lives lost, people affected, property damage), followed by tropical cyclones. In the Subcontinent, floods cause 38 per cent of disaster deaths. Droughts have caused great disruption (24 per cent of people affected during disasters) in terms of migration and loss of employment but have taken few lives. Earthquakes have been relatively low in damage because high magnitude earthquakes have been infrequent. Epidemics take large numbers of lives, but have little effect on property.9

The Maharastra study suggests that India will endure significant increases in damage caused by floods and tropical cyclones in future years. Earthquakes, epidemics, drought will be increasing challenges, but at slower rates of increase. In brief, of the natural events causing disasters, floods will remain the biggest cause of concern.

Of India's 25 states and 7 Union Territories, the following twenty-three states (plus one Territory) are particularly vulnerable to the types of disasters indicated here.10

INDIA'S VULNERABILITY					
State/Union Territory (UT)	Drought	Flood	Cyclone	Earthquake	Total
Andhra Pradesh	Yes	Yes	Yes	No	3
Arunachal Pradesh	No	Yes	No	Yes	2
Assam	No	Yes	No	Yes	2
Bihar	Yes	Yes	No	Yes	3
Gujarat	Yes	No	No	No	1
Haryana	Yes	No	No	No	1
Himachal Pradesh	No	Yes	No	Yes	2
Jammu & Kashmir	Yes	Yes	No	No	2
Karnataka	Yes	No	No	No	1
Madhya Pradesh	Yes	No	No	No	1
Maharashtra	Yes	Yes	No	Yes	3
Manipur	No	Yes	No	Yes	2
Meghalaya	No	Yes	No	Yes	2
Mizoram	No	Yes	No	Yes	2
Nagaland	No	Yes	No	Yes	2
Orissa	Yes	Yes	Yes	No	3
Punjab	Yes	Yes	No	Yes	3
Rajasthan	Yes	No	No	No	1
Sikkim	No	Yes	No	Yes	2
Tamilnadu	Yes	No	Yes	No	2
Tripura	No	Yes	No	Yes	2
Uttar Pradesh	Yes	Yes	No	Yes	3
West Bengal	Yes	Yes	Yes	Yes	4
Andaman & Nicobar (UT)	No	Yes	Yes	No	2
Totals:	14	18	5	14	

Figure I-2, India's Disaster Vulnerability. Source: Indu Prakash, Disaster Management, 36.

MANAGING DISASTERS

In responding to these kinds of hazards, India's disaster management officials and professional humanitarians conduct disaster planning and response generally within the conceptual framework of three phases: *Pre-disaster; Emergency* (or Disaster Impact); *Post Disaster* (or Recovery). Within each phase are actions to be taken, from prevention to reconstruction, and these actions are adjusted to match the type of disaster encountered. Distinctions among actions can be made when considering slow-onset disasters (drought, famine, deforestation) and rapid-onset disasters (earthquake, tsunami, tropical storm).

The Pre-disaster Phase:

Prevention is clearly achieveable when planning against man-induced disasters (witness the Bhopal incident), but such efforts may not be possible in the absolute sense when dealing with natural hazards. Still, much can be done toward prevention, such as moving a village to higher ground, out of the way of expected flood waters. This suggests the importance of risk reduction through mitigation.

Mitigation is the collective term used to encompass all actions taken prior to the occurrence of a disaster including preparedness and long-term risk reduction measures.

Preparedness consists of activities designed to minimize loss of life and damage, organizing temporary removal of people and property from a threatened location, and facilitating timely and effective rescue, relief and rehabilitation.

Early Warning is the process of monitoring situations in communities or areas known to be vulnerable to slow onset hazards, and passing the knowledge of pending hazard to people in harm's way. To be effective, warning must be related to mass education and training of the population who know what actions they must take when warned.

The Emergency Phase:

Response is the action by which extraordinary measures are taken to support human needs and to protect property. An emergency phase could be prolonged, as in a slow onset disaster such as famine, or it may be short-lived as after an earthquake.

Relief, immediately following the occurrence of a sudden disaster when measures have to be taken to search and find the survivors, includes actions to meet their basic needs for clothing, shelter, water, food and medical care.

18

Post-disaster Phase:

Rehabilitation includes measures to restore the affected community to its former living conditions (to include economic rehabilitation) while encouraging and facilitating necessary adjustments to the changes caused by the disaster.

Reconstruction includes construction of permanent housing, full restoration of all services and complete resumption of the pre-disaster state.

Disasters can throw up challenges which overwhelm the capacity of a democratic society to recover; thus they have the potential to neutralize decades of economic development and leave a country vulnerable to disease and famine. Disasters can even threaten regional stability. In the view of most disaster specialists, it is imperative that countries optimize their capabilities to help themselves and, at the same time, are in a position to assist others. An understanding of the capabilities of a country to respond to disasters is necessary for sound planning and operations by the disaster assistance responders.

To these ends, India established in 1995 a National Center for Disaster Management, and in 1998, India's Minister for Agriculture announced the formation of a National Commission on Disaster Management. A National Disaster Management Plan is now underway and is expected to be completed in 2001.[11]

By this study, the authors contribute towards an understanding of India's disaster preparedness. The study assesses its capability for self reliance and its capacity for effective response to natural and man made disasters (which also suggest its potential for assisting others). This research is of interest to humanitarians and disaster experts since any response to disasters in South Asia by Western-based organizations suggest a cooperative effort with their Indian private, non-government and Government counterparts.

In the following chapter, the authors provide an overview of India's historical problems with various hazards. Discussed are experiences with floods, famine, earthquakes and other disasters.

Endnotes

1. Tirumantiram, Tantra Seven, 9:1809.

2. Central Statistical Organisation, Department of Statistics, Ministry of Planning and Programme Implementation, *Statistical Abstract India*, 1997 (New Delhi: Government of India, 1997), 47. Also, D.M. Silveira, India Book (Bombay: Classic Publishers, 1998), 61-2, and Bryn Thomas et. al., India (Hawthorne, Australia: Lonely Planet , 1997). By the census of 1901 India's population was 238 million; in 1961 it was 439 million; in 1991 it was 846 million. With a population growing by about 2% per year, India will be the most populous country in the world by mid-21st Century.

3. The formation of the Center of Excellence (COE) in Disaster Management and Humanitarian Assistance in 1994 was a U.S. initiative that contributes to the United Nations mandate for an International Decade for Natural Disaster Reduction. See General Assembly Resolution (G.A. res.) 49/22, 49 U.N. GAOR Supp. (No. 49) at 27, U.N. Doc. A/49/49 (1994). The premise of the Resolution is that there is a close interrelationship between disaster reduction and sustainable development. The COE serves as an international training and coordinating center.

4. P.C. Sinha, ed., *Encyclopaedia of Disaster Management*, vol.1, *Introduction to Disaster Management*   (New Delhi: Anmol Publications Pvt. Ltd., 1998), 1.

5. Russell R. Dynes, *Participation in Social and Political Activities* (San Francisco: Jossey-Bass Publishers, 1980), as quoted by Maharashtra Government, Emergency Earthquake Rehabilitation Programme,   *Risk Assessment and Vulnerability Analysis* (Mumbai: July 1998), 7.

6. Sinha, 1-3.

7. Based on figures by Sinha, 4.

8. International Federation of Red Cross and Red Crescent Societies, *World Disasters Report 1998* (Bath, Somerset, UK: Oxford University Press 1998), 140.

9. Maharashtra [State] Government, *Risk Assessment and Vulnerability Analysis* (Mumbai: Government of Maharashtra, July 1998), Ch 2, 8-9.

10. Indu Prakash, *Disaster Management* (Rashtra Prahari, 1994), 36.

11. M.C. Gupta, Director, India Institute of Public Administration, and Acting Director National Center for Disaster Management, interview by authors (New Delhi: IIPA, 28 September 1998).

II. Historical Perspective

Reporting in 1925, the Royal Commission of Indian Agriculture described the Indian economy as a gamble with the monsoon. Even after decades, the gamble persists..."[1]

Rajagopalan, Management of Drought

Floods, droughts, earthquakes, cyclones and other types of disasters are taking a heavy toll of human and animal lives in India and causing enormous damage to property. The number of these disasters per year has been increasing. Here the nature and extent of these disasters is seen in a historical perspective so that there is a better appreciation of the problems in their management. This chapter provides some insight concerning the disaster hazards that have confronted the Indian people and conceptual approaches used by them to meet the disaster management challenge.

FLOODS

India is the most flood-affected country in the world after Bangladesh. There are floods almost every year in one part of the country or another, causing extensive damage to life and property. Crops, houses, public property, roads, bridges, and railway tracks are damaged and the communication channels disrupted. Flooding problems arise from heavy and concentrated rainfall, spilling of the rivers, cyclones, river erosion and drainage congestion.

Spillage of the rivers is common in almost all parts of the country. Other problems vary from area to area. Heavy and concentrated rainfall is generally experienced in the states of Uttar Pradesh, Bihar, Rajasthan and Andhra Pradesh. Cyclones cause havoc in the coastal states of Andhra Pradesh, Orissa, West Bengal, Tamilnadu and Gujarat. The steady increase in population accompanied by encroachment and deforestation and reckless developmental activities adversely affect the environment and cause extensive soil erosion. The problem of drainage congestion is experienced mostly in the flat and intensely irrigated tracts of Punjab and Haryana. It is also there in the deltaic tracts of West Bengal, Andhra Pradesh and, to some extent, in the Brahmaputra Valley of Assam.

Some of the major rivers of Bihar and West Bengal, besides, have a tendency to change their course on account of heavy sedimentation. This results in vast areas being left barren and unfit for cultivation. The

Kosi River of Bihar, known as the "River of Sorrow," has moved from its earlier bed over a distance of about 167 kms over a period of about 126 years.

The seriousness of the flood problem is illustrated by the following summary of maximum and average flood damages during the period 1953-1990.[2]

	Max.	In Year	Average
Area affected (in million hectares)	17.50	1978	7.94
Population affected (in millions)	70.45	1978	32.86
Cropped area affected (in millions)	10.15	1988	3.66
Value of crops damaged (in Rs. billions)	25.10	1988	4.48
Nos. of houses damaged (in million)	3.50	1978	1.21
Value of houses damaged (in Rs. billions)	7.41	1988	1.32
Human lives lost	11316	1977	1532
Cattle lost	618248	1979	102905
Damage to public utilities (in Rs. billions)	20.50	1985	3.47
Total damage to crops, houses & public utilities (in Rs. billions)	46.30	1988	9.37

Note: One $U.S. = about 42 Rupees (Rs.), (1998).

The five states which are most flood prone are Uttar Pradesh, Bihar, West Bengal, Assam and Orissa, but of late floods have begun to create problems in Andhra Pradesh, Rajasthan, Haryana and Gujarat also. The Government of India called upon the Central Water and Power Commission, after the 1954 floods, to draw up a Flood Control Program for the entire country.

The Central Water Commission (CWC) divides flood disaster management actions into two categories. *Pre-disaster prevention* includes flood forecasting and reservoir operations, dam safety evaluation, disaster administration, dam break modeling, legislative actions, and emergency preparedness. *Post-disaster management* includes warning procedures, emergency operations, evacuation, shelter for victims, communications systems, health operations and first aid, and immediate relief measures.[3]

The CWC takes care of flood forecasting on the inter-state rivers with 21 field divisions throughout the country. Forecasts are issued through 157 stations on the various inter-state rivers and tributaries. These forecasts are normally made 24 hours in advance and are useful to the civil and engineering authorities in arranging relief and rescue measures and for the protection of engineering structures.

The CWC began its forecasting effort in 1958, and the effort developed to provide a significant contribution toward disaster prevention capabilities in just a few years. Forecasting helped with pre-disaster management of flooding in the Delhi region during 1977-78 and again in 1988; still, destruction prevailed where forecasting was not yet implemented, such as in the Macchu Floods (Gujarat State) of 1979 and the Punjab Floods in 1988. The capability is nevertheless improving. In 1995 alone, over 5,500 forecasts were made with an accuracy of about 96 per cent. Flood forecasting has helped to facilitate the evacuation of people and cattle, removal of property, establishing relief camps, deploying boats, and mobilizing food, water, and medical care.

Flood disaster management is essentially a State responsibility. The plans are formulated, funded and executed by the State governments from their own resources on the basis of priorities fixed by them. The flood management measures could all be categorized as *structural measures* and *non-structural-measures*. For example, *structural measures* undertaken as part of India's flood management program (1991 figures) include the following tabulation, and construction continues apace.[4]

Length of embankments	15,764 kms.
Length of drainage channels	31,888 kms.
Towns protected	857
Villages raised	4705
Area benefitted	14.08 m.ha.

On-going *non-structural measures* include flood plain management, flood proofing (including disaster preparedness and response planning), flood forecasting and warning, disaster relief, flood fighting, public health measures, and flood insurance.

India's long range strategy for flood control emanated from the 1976 National Commission on Floods (*Rashtriya Barh Ayog*). The Commission made comprehensive recommendations regarding methodology, flood damage assessment, land use and regulation, cost and benefit criteria, planning and administration, financing, research, education, training and future approach. The Commission's recommendations, outlined here, continue to guide India's flood control concepts today:

- Master Plans for each basin, including the construction of storage reservoirs with multi-purpose benefits of irrigation, hydro-power generation, raising of embankments, river bank protection and river training works;
- Scientific assessments of flood damages;
- Flood plain zoning with a view to regulating the activities in the flood plain with minimum inconvenience to the people and least effect on the developmental activities;
- Liberal financing of flood control works;
- Legislation by the Central Government for regulating and developing Inter-State rivers.

Special River Commissions have been set up in states where the problem is acute. The Brahmaputra Flood Control Commission was set up for planning and implementing works in the Brahmaputra Valley and the Ganga Flood Control Commission for similar works in the Ganga Basin. The Government of India has also formulated a Model Action Plan for Disaster Preparedness for Floods and circulated that to all the State Governments and the Union Territories. The Action Plan gives a check-list of points in respect of which the entire machinery of disaster prevention and preparedness is to be energized. The State Governments are required to take action particularly on the following points:

- Setting up a Control Room (command post) and designating an agency for disaster management.
- Setting up a Coordination Committee with representatives from the India Meteorological Department, All India Radio, Social Welfare Board, Indian Red Cross Society, Army, Police, etc.
- Advance Planning for flood fighting operations covering the following points:

    Area of responsibility, organization system and allocation of duties.

    Patrols and watches along the embankment canals.

    Communication and transport facilities.

Procedure for the operation of dams and sluices.

Collection of relief and rescue materials.

Mobilization of Civil Defense and Home Guard personnel and volunteers.

Timely warning using flood warning and flood forecasting facilities.

Identifying public places where the people and livestock could be shifted.

Clearing natural drains to allow the outflow of flood waters.

Provision of medical and public health services.

The problems arising out of recurring floods, however, remain. In spite of India's considerable efforts to mitigate flood damage though its Five Year Plans and other efforts, the loss of life and property caused by flooding continues. And while wrestling with problems of too much water in some areas, the problems caused by a lack of water brings even greater challenges elsewhere.

DROUGHTS AND FAMINES

India's dry regions encompass some 94 million hectares and one-third (300 million) of the Indian people. Typically, half of the dry areas in India are affected by drought every four years. In last quarter of the 20th Century, India has moved away from relief strategies to programs for mitigation and food self-sufficiency to counter the drought problem.[5]

Drought is considered a "creeping" hazard because it develops over a period of months and has a prolonged life - sometimes several months or even years. It is not confined to a particular area and its impact may extend over several thousand square kilometers. It is comparable to long term environmental degradation and, at times, it is difficult to tell where drought ends and human-induced desertification begins. Over-grazing, poor cropping methods, deforestation and improper soil conservation techniques may not, by themselves, create drought but they are illustrative of drought related disaster.

Drought is generally of the following three types:

Meteorological drought when there is a significant decrease (more than 25 per cent) from normal precipitation over an area.

Hydrological drought which is the result of prolonged meteorological drought and is characterized by depletion of surface water and consequent drying up of lakes, rivers and reservoirs, affecting irrigation and power generation.

Agricultural drought which occurs when soil moisture and rainfall are inadequate during the sowing season, affecting the crops.

India has been affected by drought and resultant famine in the past, particularly during the pre-independence years. As a matter of fact, till 1947 when India became independent, famine relief policy applied to all types of natural disasters.

According to the *Encyclopedia of Disaster Management* edited by P.C. Sinha, "the sub-continent has suffered at least a dozen great famines in which a million or more people have died in the past 1,000 years; there have been four major famines in the last 100 years."[6] Sinha and others attribute drought in the country to the following major causes:

- El Niño effect, the periodic appearance of warm and saline oceanic currents in the eastern pacific west of Peru;

- A negative swing in the South Oscillation Index which measures the difference in the pressure between Port Darwin in northern Australia and Tahiti in French Polynesia;

- A combination of El Niño and the South Oscillation Index known as ENSO.

ENSO is considered the most notable and pronounced example of global climatic variability on the inter annual time scale. It owes its existence to large scale ocean atmospheric interactions in the equatorial Pacific. The world's most extensive region of warm water is located in the western tropical Pacific-Indonesian region. The heavy rainfall and associated heating of atmosphere over this huge "Warm Pool" is a major source of atmospheric heating which drives the large scale circulations. It leads to massive dislocation of the rainfall in the tropics, bringing drought to large areas and torrential rains to otherwise arid regions.

The government policy on drought relief has evolved over a period from the various measures adopted for amelioration of distress caused by famines and scarcities from time to time. The famine policy of the earliest rulers depended on their concern for the welfare of the people and the resources of the State. Kautilya, the great philosopher, wrote more than 2000 years ago that in the event of occurrence of famine a good king should institute the building of forts and water-works with the grant of food, or share (his) provisions (with them), or entrust the country to another king. Mohammed Bin Tughlaq took vigorous measures to alleviate the effects of drought which occurred in 1343 AD during his regime. The Mughal Emperor Shah Jahan is also known to have distributed money during the famine in 1630 AD.

Famines became a recurring feature of the country during the rule of the East India Company followed by that of the British Government. In the about 90 year period from 1765, when the East India Company took over the Diwani of Bengal to 1858, the country experienced twelve famines and four severe scarcities. The frequency of famines increased further during the first fifty years of direct British rule over the country. Between 1860 and 1908, famine or scarcity prevailed in one part of the country or the other in twenty out of the total forty-nine years. The thirteen years from 1896 to 1908 was a period of unmitigated disaster for the country when, except for in 1898 and 1904, there were famine or scarcity conditions in one part of the country or another. These famines were essentially the result of economic exploitation of the country by the colonial rulers.[7]

Three famine commissions were appointed by the British till the end of the 19th century. The first Famine Commission circulated a Famine Code to the provincial governments, embodying the principles and procedures for the administration of relief. The second Famine Commission recommended that small as well as large works should be taken up at the district level as soon as the situation deteriorated. It favored the payment of wages by results subject to a minimum and maximum daily wage. The Commission also recommended a more positive policy in the suspension and remission of land revenue. The third Famine Commission warned the government against the danger of being caught unawares and emphasized that a complete and authoritative plan for relief be drawn up. The plan should include program of public and village works, provision of adequate tools and implements, and grant of liberal advances to agriculturists in the initial stages itself. For the preservation of cattle, the Commission recommended cultivation of fodder crops, grant of loan for purchase of fodder and opening of cattle camps.

The Famine Codes were useful in tackling situations created by local crop failures, but they were ineffective in the face of large scale famines. The Bengal famine of 1943, when no less than 1.5 million people died, was unprecedented in its tragic dimensions. It was the inevitable consequence of government's failure to take any steps to meet the dislocation in production, supply and distribution of food-grains in the wake of the World War II.

After independence, it was felt that the Codes needed to be revised keeping in view the social and economic goals of the welfare state. During the fifties and the sixties, the Famine Relief Codes were gradually replaced by Scarcity Relief Manuals. Scarcity was defined as a marked deterioration of the agricultural season due to the failure of rains or floods and damage to crops from insects resulting in severe unemployment and consequent distress among the agricultural labor and small cultivators. The manuals made provision for dealing with all kinds of natural calamities including drought. They prescribed measures to provide reasonable purchasing power to the affected people and ensure the availability of goods and services. The more recent manuals lay down measures not only to alleviate distress but also suggest alternative arrangements for crop production, better water management and creation of assets through employment generation works.

During the last nearly fifty years, the country experienced drought in varying degrees in the following years:[8]

Year	% Area of the Country affected	Category
1951	33.2	Moderate
1952	25.8	Slight
1965	42.9	Moderate
1966	32.3	Moderate
1968	20.6	Slight
1969	19.9	Slight
1971	13.3	Slight
1972	44.4	Severe
1974	29.3	Moderate
1979	39.4	Moderate
1982	33.1	Moderate
1985	30.1	Moderate
1986	19.0	Slight
1987	49.2	Severe

The experience of successive disasters has brought about qualitative improvements in the disaster management efforts. During the drought of 1965-66, India required over 10 million tons of grain from outside sources to meet the demands for feeding its people. It prompted the building up of a reliable Public Distribution System (PDS) to take care of the food emergencies. The drought of 1972 witnessed the adoption of employment generating schemes to enhance the purchasing power of the people. The drought of 1979 underlined the need to create durable and productive assets to enable the people withstand future calamities with greater resilience. During the drought of 1987, successful mitigation efforts reduced the impact upon the people, and a conscious effort to maintain the quality of life of the affected people proved effective. Here the focus was on providing food, clean drinking water and health care.[9]

The Government of India issued fresh guidelines in 1989 to revise the relief manuals on drought management. The policy now is directed more towards mitigation and is preventive in nature rather than merely curative. The relief measures are not conceived in isolation but integrated with the development ethos and programs under the Five Year Plans. The areas prone to periodic droughts have been identified and programs formulated for the prevention of droughts in those areas under the 'Drought Prone Area Program' (DPAP). The National Rural Employment Programs (NREP) and Rural Landless Employment Guarantee Programs (RLEGP) are launched to serve as anti-poverty interventions and also as employment support measures in the years of crop failure.

Today, the operational approach to combating drought in India includes the following activities: *early warning* (monitoring meteorological, hydrological, and agricultural conditions to give response a head start); *preparedness measures* (health, veterinary, water disaster assistance planning); *water conservation* (budgeting and additional supply); *stabilizing crop production* (alternative crops, seed reserves, saving crops); *food security* (food where needed at reasonable costs); and *employment generation* (including preserving the farm and its assets).

While drought and floods allow for some warning and response, earthquakes strike unannounced. They cause great destruction in just a short time.

EARTHQUAKES

About two-thirds of India lies in seismic zones of moderate to severe intensity. Over half of the Indian sub-continent is vulnerable to earthquakes. Just as earthquake-prone areas have been identified and demarcated as such all over the world, India has also been divided into different zones as per Indian Standards (IS) Code 1893-1975 (third revision). These codes provide guidance for designing and constructing earthquake resistant structures within different zone designations. The Disaster Management Institute (of Bhopal) manual on *Earthquake Disaster Management* lists the seismic regions of India:

- Kashmir and Western Himalayas;
- Central Himalayas (including Nepal, Himalayas);
- North-East India;
- Indo-Gangetic Basin and Rajasthan;
- Cambay and the Rann of Kutch;
- Peninsular India;
- Andaman and Nicobar Islands.[11]

The potential for earthquakes to affect the Indian people is significant. Earthquake, in a sense, is the most disastrous of all natural calamities because it catches the people unawares. Though it is now possible to predict its occurrence in a region, precise prediction in terms of time and place is still a difficult task.

The major earthquakes which have caused devastation in the Indian sub-continent during the last two centuries are tabulated below:[12]

Year	Location	Magnitude on Richter Scale	Remarks
1803	Kumaon region	6.5	300 persons killed.
1828	Near Srinagar, J&K	6	Number of persons killed 100; houses destroyed 1,200.
1869	Cachar, Assam	7.5	Earth fissures and sand craters; Investigated by T.Oldham, led to his compiling a catalogue of quakes.
1885	A few miles west of Srinagar	7	35,000 lives lost of which 3,500 were human beings.
1897	Shillong plateau (Assam)	8.7	Oldham's earthquake described earlier
1905	Kangra (HP)	8.5	Kangra, Dharamshala and neighborhood ruined completely; about 20,000 persons killed.
1918	Srimangal (Assam)	7.6	Area of 4,500 sq. Km. suffered heavy damage.
1930	Dhubri (Assam)	7.1	Railway culverts and bridges damaged.

Figure II-1, Earthquake Examples. Source: A.K.R. Hemmady, *Earthquakes*, 61-3.

Figure II-1 (continued)			
Year	Location	Magnitude on Richter Scale	Remarks
1934	Bihar-Nepal border	8.3	About 10,000 lives lost.
1943	Assam	7.2	Destruction over north-east Assam.
1947	North-east of Jammu	6	Serious material damage at Bhadarwah.
1947	Assam	7.75	Damage caused at Dibrugarh, Jorhat and Tezpur.
1950	Tibet	8.5	One of the disastrous earthquakes in history; 156 casualties due to earthquakes and landslides, 532 due to consequent floods.
1958	Himachal Pradesh/ Tibet border	6.3	Rupture of ground and a few landslides in an area of 150 sq.km. around Kapkote with cracking of buildings.
1963	33.9°, 74.7°E Badagaum	5.3	79 killed, 400 injured.
1966	Nepal-India border	6.1	80 killed.
1975	Kinnaur (HP)	6.8	44 people killed.
1980	India-Nepal border	6.1	About 200 people killed; damage to buildings at Dharchulla and Pithoragarh.
1980	Jammu	5.2	15 people died; damage to houses at Kathua.
1982	Dhanbad	6.5	Details not available.
1988	Nepal	6.5	About 1,000 people killed.
1988	Manipur-Burma	7.1	Little damage; three persons killed.
1991	Uttarkashi	n/a	Considerable damage.
1993	Delhi	6.5	Not much damage.

Indian disaster management planners have developed specific activities within the cycle of disaster management phases briefly mentioned in Chapter 1 (pre-disaster, emergency, post disaster) to tackle earthquake-generated problems. Experience has shown these problems tend to fall within the broad categories (such as administrative, technical, medical, and psychological), and that they can be effectively handled throughout the disaster cycle.[13]

In the *Pre-disaster phase* efforts are made to develop earthquake prediction and warning processes, but the results have been imprecise. The psychological dimensions of such a system would require accuracy in the assessment combined with an information program for potentially affected people so that they might react in appropriate ways when given warning. Hazard assessment is important for assessing the frequency and magnitude of earthquakes and, therefore, developing vulnerability and damage estimates. This assists efforts to reduce the impact of earthquake hazards on the community. Mitigation measures (structural and nonstructural) include the construction of earthquake-resistant structures, retrofitting existing structures, and efforts such as developing earthquake codes and hazard zoning, and public awareness campaigns.

Emergency phase actions might include rescuing trapped persons, evacuating and treating of victims, and providing shelter for those whose housing has been destroyed. Providing food, clean water and subsistence supplies (clothing, hygiene kits, cooking utensils, plastic sheeting) has proven helpful to reduce the need for mass evacuation from the affected area. Additional activities that have proven necessary are maintaining law and order, health and sanitation regimes and facilities and a public information program. Counseling and spiritual support are an important aspect of maintaining public morale.

The *Post-disaster* phase includes engineering and technical studies (along with seismological studies of aftershocks) necessary for recording damage, estimating insurance payments, evaluating structural designs. This leads the way for repairing buildings and demolishing others. During this phase, new homes may be built on site or whole villages may be relocated. Psychological dimensions can be seen as panic attacks, rumors, alcoholism, school droop-out and low morale. Thus, new and rebuilt dwellings provided to the public after earthquakes may well go unoccupied because of psychological trauma and fear of yet another earthquake—hence a preference to remain in temporary shelters.[14] Also a part of the psychological dimension is the need to create job opportunities for the mental health of affected victims as well as the health of their local economy. Indian disaster management professionals also assert that a critical action in this phase is to review contingency plans, design standards, training needs, and other practices to improve future capabilities and capacities for managing disasters.

Earthquake mitigation measures receive special attention in India and deserve additional comment here. A seismic (hazard) zoning map has been prepared by the Indian Standards Institution in the light of earthquake occurrences, the maximum intensities reached and the maximum probable intensities that could be caused in various areas of the country in future earthquakes depending on the seismogenic-tectonic features of the area. This should aid planning against future earthquake hazards.

The India Meteorological Department (IMD) is the nodal agency for monitoring the earthquakes. It maintains 56 seismological stations, five regional meteorological offices and 32 seismological observatories in different parts of India. There are also a number of temporary observatories at various project sites in different states.

In the field of structural mitigation research and development, the Department of Earthquake Engineering of University of Roorkee has done exhaustive work in evolving measures for suitable strengthening of buildings against seismic forces of variable magnitude. Extensive research has been undertaken on the 'Strengthening of Low Strength Masonry' (LSM) at the Department of Earthquake Engineering, University of Roorkee. Besides, to improve the durability and performance of mud houses, particularly their resistance to seismic forces, some innovative techniques of design and construction have been evolved. The National Building Organization (NBO) under the Ministry of Urban Development has also been planning and promoting the design and construction of earthquake resistant buildings/houses through Experimental Housing Projects.

CYCLONES

The word 'cyclone' is derived from the Greek work 'cyclos' meaning the coils of a snake. The tropical storms in the Bay of Bengal and in the Arabian Sea give the appearance of the coiled serpents of sea, and so they were called 'cyclones.' These storms are known by different names in different parts of the world. They are called typhoons in Western North Pacific and China Seas, hurricanes in Western North Atlantic, Eastern North Pacific and Western South Pacific, *Baguios* in the Philippine region, *Willy Willies* in the Australian waters, and as cyclones in the Arabian Sea, Bay of Bengal and the Southern Indian Ocean.

Some of the severe cyclones which took a heavy toll of lives and property in the states of Andhra Pradesh and Orissa during the last fifty years, and recently in Gujarat, were as follows:[15]

Andhra Pradesh

27.11.1949	Near Machilipatnam	Wind speed reached 100 km. per hour. Tidal waves of 3 to 5 mts. in height inundated the coast to a depth of 15 kms. A million acre paddy crops were submerged. About 800 people died and thousands were rendered homeless.
7.11.1969	Near Kakinada	Took a toll of about 900 lives. Property worth nearly Rs. one billion was damaged.
19.11.1977	Near Chirala	Tidal waves reached 5.5 mts. In height and inundated the coast to a depth of 25 kms. About 10,000 human lives and 6,00,000 cattle were lost. Property worth about Rs. two billion was damaged.
14.11.1984	Kotapatnam, Nellore District	Winds of 200 kmph and water killed 625 people and left 200,000 people homeless. Property loss was Rs. 650 million.

Orissa

9.10.1967	Orissa coast between Puri and Paradeep	The severe cyclonic storm caused extensive devastation in coastal Orissa. The death toll was about 1,000 persons and 50,000 cattle. Property worth billions was damaged.
30.10.1971	Near Paradeep	The tidal wave went inland over a distance of 15 to 25 kms, completely destroying the standing crops. About 10,000 human lives and 1,00,000 cattle were lost. Property worth about Rs. 300 crores was damaged.

Gujarat

9.6.1998	Kandla Port, Kutch District	Winds touching 200 kmph and tidal waves destroy Kandla Port, killing over 4,000. In spite of early warning by the Meteorological Department, Kutch District Administration does not react with timely warning to people.

Figure II-2, Examples of Cyclone Disasters. Source: P.C. Sinha, ed., *Encyclopaedia of Disaster Management*, Vol 7, "Wind and Water Driven Disasters," p. 170; K.S. Ramesh, "Cyclone Disaster Management in Coastal Districts of Andhra Pradesh–A Case Study," *Disaster Management*, pp. 159-77; *Outlook* (July 6, 1998), p. 50; *India Today* (June 22 1998), p. 31.

Cyclones fall into three general categories. The *wave cyclone* of middle and high latitudes (also called extra-tropical cyclone) ranges in severity from a weak disturbance to a powerful storm. The *tropical cyclone* of low latitude over ocean areas ranges from a mild disturbance to the terribly destructive hurricane or typhoon. The *tornado* is an intense cyclonic vortex of enormously powerful winds.

India has developed an elaborate cyclone warning system to meet the cyclone threat. It is one of the important responsibilities of the India Meteorological Department. The warnings are issued by the Area Cyclone Warning Centers (ACWC) located at Calcutta, Madras and Bombay, and Cyclone Warning Centers (CWC) at Bhubaneshwar, Visakhapatnam and Ahmedabad. The Meteorological Office at New Delhi issues cyclone warning bulletins and cyclone advisories via the All India Radio and Doordarshan (a National TV network) for the North Indian Ocean to Bangladesh, Myanmar, Maldives, Pakistan, Sri Lanka, Thailand and India. This office also issues cyclone advisories for tropical cyclones in the South-West Indian Ocean to Mauritius. The cyclones are tracked with the help of regular observation from the network of surface and air stations, cyclone detection radars, satellites, and reports furnished by ships and aircraft.[16]

The country has a network of ten cyclone detection radars which have been set up all along the coast. Six of these are located at Calcutta, Paradip, Visakhapatnam, Machilipatnam, Madras and Karaikal on the east coast while the remaining four are located at Cochin, Goa, Bombay and Bhuj on the west coast. The range of these radars is 400 kms.

Satellites have been found very dependable in tracking the weather systems. When the cyclone is beyond the range of the coastal radar, its intensity and movement are monitored with the help of weather satellites. The India Meteorological Department has the capability to monitor half hourly cloud pictures from the Indian Geostationary Satellite INSAT-1D and from the Polar Orbiting Satellites launched by USA and Russia.

The states of Andhra Pradesh, Orissa, Tamilnadu and West Bengal on the east coast are prone to severe cyclones, though Kerala, Karnataka, Maharashtra, and Gujarat on the west coast also experience the fury of cyclones. The Andaman and Nicobar island and the Lakshdweep are also vulnerable. It is estimated that nearly ten per cent of the world's tropical cyclones originate over the Bay of Bengal and the Arabian Sea. Of these, the majority have their genesis over the Bay of Bengal and they strike the eastern coast of India.

The measures taken to deal with cyclones could be classified under three heads depending on whether they are short term, medium term or long term. *Short Term* measures involve contingency plans, regular warnings, evacuation from vulnerable areas and public health and sanitation measures. *Medium Term* measures can include developing communications networks for early warning, public education and arranging for emergency stores and first aid centers. *Long Term* measures include strengthening houses, land planning and regulation to reduce the risks and planting trees around houses to serve as wind and tide breakers.

Contingency plans have been evolved by the state governments to deal with the situations arising out of cyclones. In Andhra Pradesh, for example, there is a Standing Committee under the Chief Secretary of the State entrusted with the overall responsibility for disaster preparedness. The operational functions are undertaken by the revenue department. The plan includes identification of villages within a specified distance from the coast or within a specified distance along the disaster prone belt; location of concrete buildings outside the reach of disaster; setting up free kitchen facilities; mobilizing the available transport; charting out the evacuation routes; and locating markets for the various needs and requirements of the affected people. As a permanent rehabilitation measure, construction of more than one hundred thousand cyclone proof houses has been taken up by the State Government on a priority basis in a 20 km belt along the coast. A special Housing Corporation has been set up for the purpose.

The Government of Tamilnadu have an Anti-Disaster Plan to meet the challenge of disasters like cyclones. This plan, together with the pre-disaster preparatory measures taken at the instance of Member for Natural Calamities, Board of Revenue, have enhanced the capability of the coastal districts to face disasters.

In Orissa, the Board of Revenue is responsible for all kinds of relief operations, and a Member of the Board functions as the Relief Commissioner. There are Natural Calamities Committee in each district to deal with situations arising out of natural disasters and take the appropriate decisions and relief measures with promptitude.

In some states, at the initiative of the Meteorological Department, Cyclone Distress Mitigation Committees have been set up. These bring together on a common platform the disaster managers, civil, police and military officials, communication managers and the meteorologists.

OTHER DISASTERS

Apart from the major disasters discussed above, there are some other disasters also of a comparatively minor nature. *Landslides* are a frequent occurrence in the hill ranges of India. They take place in the Himalayas, the north-eastern hill ranges, western ghats, eastern ghats, Nilgiris and the Vindhyas. Landslides cause extensive damage to the roads, buildings, forests, plantations and agricultural fields. Lately, they caused havoc in the hill districts of Uttar Pradesh, wiping out entire villages.

Avalanches take place in the high altitude regions of Western Himalayas. They cause great hardship to people living in those remote areas.

Volcanic activity is rare in India, though in one of the islands in the Bay of Bengal east of the Andamans there is a dormant volcano which erupted around the year 1800.

India, it has been said, is "a land of disasters."[17] It is not possible to predict or prevent all the different kinds of natural disasters. A state of preparedness and ability to respond quickly to a natural calamity can, however, considerably mitigate the loss of life and property and human suffering, and restore normalcy within a short period. It is therefore of paramount importance that a plan of action for dealing with the contingencies which arise in the wake of natural calamities is formulated and periodically updated.

It is a matter of satisfaction that the Government of India as well as the State Governments are now paying much greater attention to disaster management and that plans to deal with different kinds of calamities are being formulated at the national, state and local levels. The following chapter provides basic information that can be of help to disaster management officials and private volunteer organizations concerned with disaster contingency planning for India.

Endnotes

1. V. Rajagopalan, "Management of Drought," *The Training of Trainers Programme on Drought Management* (New Delhi: National Centre for Disaster Management, Indian Institute of Public Administration, 1997), 4.

2. Vinod K. Sharma, Program Director, National Centre for Disaster Management, *Training Program on Flood and Landslides Management* (New Delhi: Indian Institute of Public Administration, 1997), 12-14. Tabulations provided herein by the India Central Water Commission.

3. G. S. Chandpuri, H.S. Saxena, and D. S. Khangura, Central Water Commission, "Flood Disaster Management," *Training Program on Flood and Landslides Management,* (New Delhi: Indian Institute of Public Administration, 1997), 2-1 through 2-5.

4. M. L. Baweja, Central Water Commission, "Flood Disaster Mitigation Practice in India," *Training Program on Flood and Landslides Management,* (New Delhi: Indian Institute of Public Administration, 1997), 5.

5. Department of Humanitarian Affairs, United Nations, "1997 World Disaster Reduction Campaign–Information Kit, Drought: What Can Be Done About Drought"; available from <www.quipu.net/seminars/risk97/English/day/kit/lessons.html>, Internet; accessed 18 November 1998.

6. P. C. Sinha, 116.

7. B. M. Bhatia, *Famines in India: A Study in some Aspects of the Economic History of India, 1860-1965* (Asia Publishing House, 1967), 8, 238.

8. Government of India, *Yojana* (16-30 June 1989): 8.

9. Department of Humanitarian Affairs, United Nations.

10. Disaster Management Institute, *Earthquake Disaster Management* (Bhopal: DMI, October 1996), 6.

11. Disaster Management Institute, *Earthquake Disaster Management*(Bhopal: DMI, 1996), 11.

12. A. K. R. Hemmady, *Earthquakes* (New Delhi: National Book Trust, 1966), 61-3.

13. Sinha, Vol. 6, *Geological and Mass Movement Disasters*, 140-1. Sinha lists administrative challenges as mobilizing relief workers and supplies, extricating victims, disposal of remains, law and order, unemployment and rehabilitation. Technical problems might include structural damage, damage to communications facilities, water pipe lines, water tanks, and pollution. Medical problems are initially first aid, then evacuation of casualties, treatment, disease and possible epidemic. There is the potential for damage to hospitals and the routes to them.

14. P. V. Unnikrishnan, M.D. Oxfam (India) Trust, interview by authors (New Delhi: 23 September 1998). See also, Disaster Management Institute, *Earthquake Disaster Managemen* t (Bhopal: DMI, 1996), 30.

15. P.C. Sinha, Vol. 7, *Wind and Water Driven Disasters*, 170; K.S. Ramesh, "Cyclone Disaster Management in Coastal Districts of Andhra Pradesh–A Case Study," *Disaster Management* , ed., Vinod K. Sharma (New Delhi: National Centre for Disaster Management, 1997), pp. 159-77; *Outlook* (6 July 1998): 50; *India Today* (22 June 1998): 31.

16. G. S. Mandal, Deputy Director General, India Meteorological Department, "Cyclone Forecasting and Warning Systems," *Training of Trainers Programme on Disaster Management for NGOs,* ed. by Vinod K. Sharma (New Delhi: Indian Institute of Public Administration, 1997), p. TP-6.

17. Aroon Purie, *India Today* (7 September 1998):1.

III. Planning Factors:
Land, People, and Infrastructure

It's appalling, that in a country where more than 60 million people are affected by disasters every year, there is no policy on disaster management. It's ad hoc and haphazard, what food to distribute, what medicines to supply, how to prevent the outbreak of epidemics — such questions are never addressed.[1]

Dr. P. V. Unnikrishnan of OXFAM

This chapter provides background information that can be useful to disaster management planners in India. It can assist private volunteer and other international organizations that may be positioned to compliment India's efforts, and to those who might request Indian advice and assistance for disasters elsewhere. What follows is a synopsis of issues concerning India's geographic situation, its population and infrastructure. The information is based upon Indian source material and the work of Indian disaster management experts.

India is one of the world's oldest civilisations with rich cultural heritage. It covers an area of 3,287,590 square kilometers, extending from the snow-covered Himalayan heights to the tropical rain forests of the south. Planning considerations begin with a review of the geography.

THE SUBCONTINENT: GEOGRAPHY AND GEOLOGY

The seventh largest country of the world, India is well-marked off from the rest of Asia by mountains and seas, which give the country a distinct geographical entity. Bounded by the Great Himalayas in the north, it stretches southwards and, at the Tropic of Cancer, tapers off into the Indian Ocean between the Bay of Bengal on the east and the Arabian Sea on the west.

The Land

Lying entirely in the northern hemisphere, the mainland extends between latitudes 8°4' and 37°6' north, longitudes 68°7' and 97°25' east and measures about 3,214 kms from north to south between the extreme latitudes and about 2,933 kms from east to west between the extreme longitudes. It has a land frontier of about 15,200 kms and a coast line, including the Andaman and Nicobar Islands and the Lakshadweep, of 7,516.6 kms.

India has Afghanistan and Pakistan to the north-west, China, Bhutan and Nepal to the north, and Myanmar and Bangladesh to the east. It is separated from Sri Lanka by a narrow channel of sea formed by the Palk Strait and the Gulf of Mannar.

The rivers of India could be classified as (i) Himalayan rivers (ii) Peninsular rivers (iii) Coastal rivers and (iv) rivers of the inland drainage basin. The Himalayan rivers are perennial as they are generally snow-fed and have reasonable flow throughout the year.

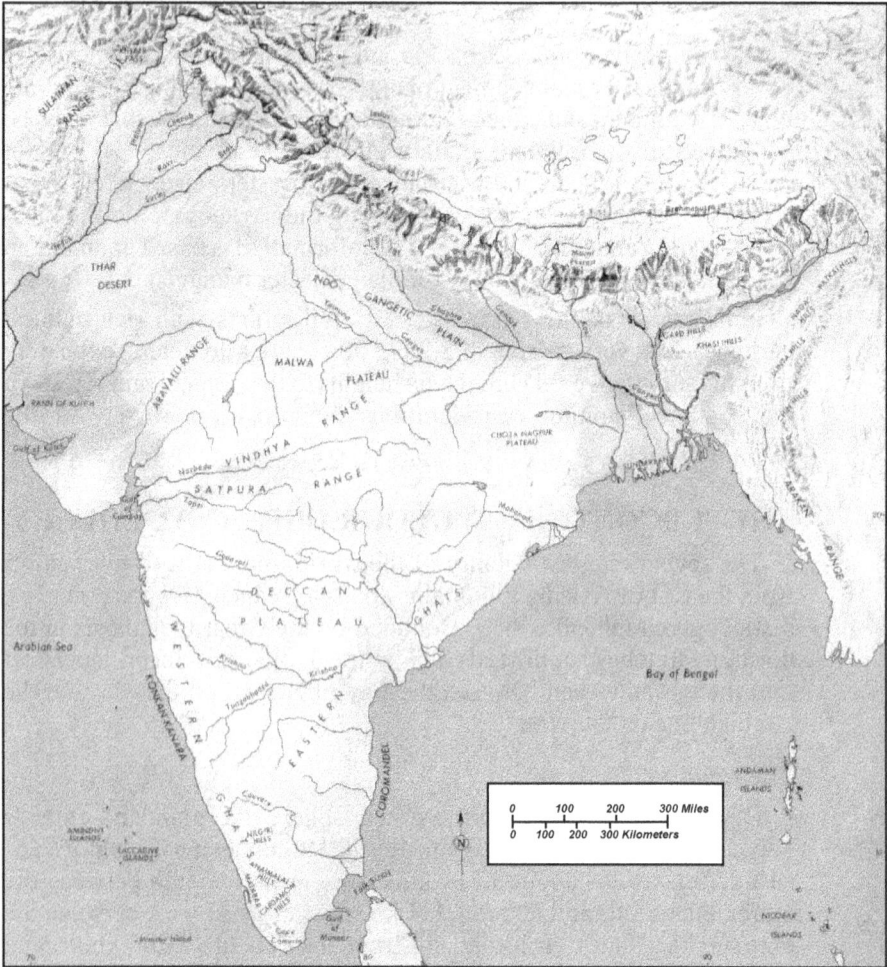

Figure III-1, Section of Southwest Asia. Source: *India A Country Study*. Washington: Library of Congress, 1986.

During the monsoon, the Himalayas receive very heavy rainfall and the rivers discharge the maximum quantity of water, causing frequent floods. The Peninsular rivers are generally rain-fed and, therefore, fluctuate in volume. The coastal streams, especially on the west coast, are short in length and have limited catchment areas. Most of them are flashy and non-perennial. The streams of the inland drainage basin of western Rajasthan are few and far between. Most of them are of an ephemeral character. They drain towards the individual basins or salt lakes like the Sambhar or are lost in the sands having no outlet to the sea. The Luni is the only river of this category that drains into the Rann of Kutch.[2]

The Ganga sub-basin is the largest in India receiving waters from an area which comprise about one quarter of the total area of the country. Its boundaries are defined by the Himalayas in the north and Vindhyas in the south. The Ganga flows through UP, Bihar and West Bengal in India and thereafter enters Bangladesh. It is joined by a number of smaller Himalayan rivers including the Yamuna, Ghagra, Gomti, Gandak and Kosi. The important rivers flowing north from central India into the Ganga/Yamuna are the Chambal, Betwa and Sone.

The Brahmaputra and the Barak flowing from east to west in the north-eastern region are international rivers with immense water resources potential. The Godavari in the southern Peninsula has the second largest river basin. Next to it is the Krishna basin followed by the Mahanadi basin.

The climate of India may be broadly described as tropical monsoon type. There are four seasons: (I) winter (January-February), (ii) hot weather summer (March-May), (iii) rainy south-western monsoon (June-September), and (iv) post-monsoon, also known as north-east monsoon in the southern Peninsula (October-December). The climate is affected by two seasonal winds - the north-east monsoon and the south-west monsoon. The north-east monsoon commonly known as winter monsoon blows from land to sea whereas the south-west monsoon known as summer monsoon blows from sea to land after crossing the Indian Ocean, the Arabian Sea and the Bay of Bengal. The south-west monsoon brings much of the rainfall in the country. With the improvements in meteorology, it is now possible to make forecasts about the monsoon rains.

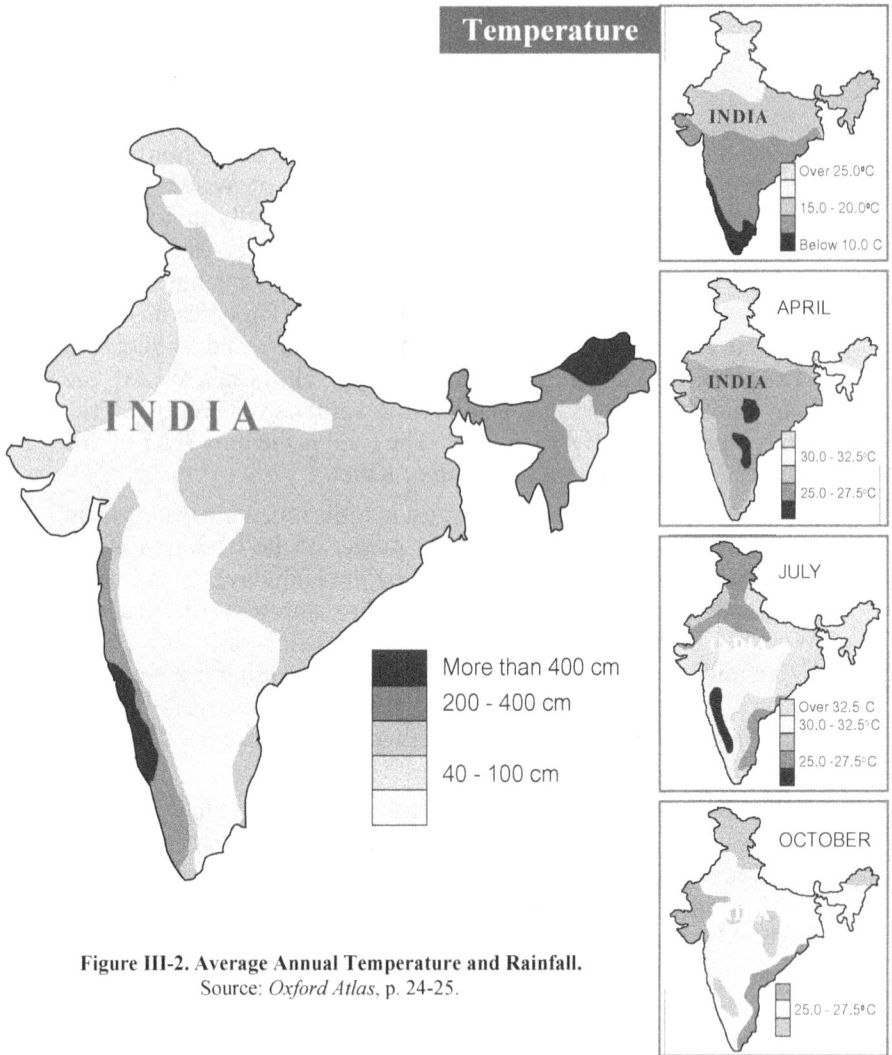

Temperature

INDIA

Over 25.0°C
15.0 - 20.0°C
Below 10.0 C

APRIL

INDIA

30.0 - 32.5°C
25.0 - 27.5°C

JULY

Over 32.5 C
30.0 - 32.5°C
25.0 -27.5°C

OCTOBER

25.0 - 27.5°C

More than 400 cm
200 - 400 cm
40 - 100 cm

Figure III-2. Average Annual Temperature and Rainfall.
Source: *Oxford Atlas*, p. 24-25.

Geologically, the Indian subcontinent is divided into three principal segments. These are the:

- Himalayas and their extension to the east and the west;
- Indo-Gangetic Plains to the south; and
- Peninsular India.

The Himalayas and the mountain chains that extend beyond them are made up mainly of Proterozoic and Phanerozoic sediments, largely marine, and are tectonically highly disturbed. They owe their origin to diastrophic movements which brought these mountains into existence in comparatively recent geological times. They are characterized by highly folded and faulted rocks, and attain enormous heights.

46

The Indo-Gangetic unit is a very young feature, formed during the Quaternary Period. It has little to show by way of high relief and generally consists of undulating plains carved by highly developed river systems. Its surface is covered by sediments of the Holocene or Recent age. On the west, it includes the vast stretch of the Thar Desert.

The Indian Peninsula is entirely unlike the two preceding divisions, both geologically and physiographically. It is a stable mass of Precambrian rocks, some of which have been there since the formation of the Earth. These rock masses have remained in position throughout their geological history with hardly any structural changes. Among the few Phanerozoic events to affect the Peninsula are the sedimentation during the Gondwana times and the Mesozoic era along with the outpouring of the Deccan lavas. The topography of the Peninsula is rugged, though not like that of the Himalayas. The peninsular mountains, except for the Aravalli Range, do not owe their origin to tectonism but to denudation of the pre-existing plateaus leaving relict chains - they are the mountains of circumdenudation.

There is yet a fourth division, though not so well marked. These are the coastal plains surrounding the Peninsula together with the continental margins on their front. These are made up entirely of Recent or Holocene sediments which sometimes cover Phanerozoic strata of great geological importance.

POPULATION

India's population, as of the 1991 Census, stood at 846.30 million. The second most populous country of the world, India is home to 16 per cent of world's population even though the country has only 2.42 per cent of the total world area. The United Nations Population Fund in its *The State of World Population* , 1998 has stated that India is rapidly climbing the population ladder and, with a higher birth rate, it would overtake the most populous country China by 2050 AD. The world population, according to the Report, is growing by over 80 million a year with India contributing about one-fifth to that growth. For comparison, here are selected countries and their projected growth to year 2050.

Population of Selected Countries (In Thousands)

Year	Brazil	China	India	Indonesia	Nigeria	Pakistan	Russia	USA
1998	165,851	1,255,698	982,233	206,338	106,409	148,166	147,434	277,028
2050	244,230	1,477,730	1,528,853	311,857	244,311	345,484	121,256	349,318

Figure III-3, Population of Selected Countries. Source: United Nations, Department of Economic and Social Affairs, Population Division; Internet.

Looking at the population scenario in a historical perspective, one finds that during the earlier decades of the century, India's population was characterised by high birth rate, high death rate, high infant mortality rate, maternal mortality rate and low expectancy of life. After independence, programs to control killer diseases like malaria, cholera and plague, and the steady improvement in public hygiene and nutritional status of the population led to the death rate and infant mortality rate falling two-fold or even more and the life expectancy at birth being nearly doubled. The birth rate also declined from 40.8 in 1951 to 27.4 in 1996, but this has not been enough to offset the additions as result of decreasing death rate and infant mortality rate as far as the total population of the country is concerned. The net result is that about 15.5 million people are currently being added to the country's population every year.[3]

India's population has, in fact, multiplied more than four times during the century. It was 238 million in 1901, when the country was undivided, increased to 846 million in 1991, and is presently estimated to be around 976 million. This continuing increase in population has very serious social and economic implications. Tensions within the society are likely to exacerbate. The unemployment situation would worsen. The environment would be under tremendous pressure with the carrying capacity of land being exceeded.[4]

The Family Planning Program was started in the country as far back as 1951 as a purely demographic program. Subsequently, the element of public education and extension was included to facilitate outcomes under the program. During the seventies, the program unfortunately received a setback when coercive methods were employed in pursuance of a target-based approach. It was revived as a voluntary exercise, the government's main effort being to provide services on the one hand and encourage the citizens through information, education and communication on the other hand to use such services. Experience has shown that health of women in the reproductive age group of small children is of crucial importance in tackling the problem of increasing population. There has thus been a change in approach from Family Planning to Family Welfare. From the Central Government's Seventh Plan (1984-89) onwards, the programs have evolved with focus on the health needs of women in the reproductive age group and of children below the age of five years, and on providing contraceptives and spacing services to the desirous people. The objective is to stabilise the population at a level consistent with the needs of national development.[5]

Population Growth of India, Projected to 2016 (In Millions)

	(1)	(2)	(3)	(4)	(5)	(6)	(7)	(8)	(9)	(10)	(11)	(12)	(13)	(14)	(15)
Year	1901	1911	1921	1931	1941	1951	1961	1971	1981	1991	1996	2001	2006	2011	2016
Population	238	252	251	279	319	361	439	548	683	846	934	1012	1094	1179	1264

Figure III-4, Population Growth. Source: *Statistical Outline of India, 1997-98* (Mumbai: Tata Donnelley Ltd., December 1997), 37; also *Statistical Abstract India 1997* (New Delhi: Central Statistical Organization, December 1997), 29.

Population growth nevertheless remains one of India's most critical problems. The population density has gone up from 216 in 1981 to 267 persons per sq. km. in 1991 (excluding Assam and Jammu &Kashmir). The 10 heavily populated districts of the country are Calcutta, Chennai, Greater Mumbai, Hyderabad, Delhi, Chandigarh, Mahe, Howrah, Kanpur City and Bangalore. All of them have density of above 2,000 persons per square kilometer and 5.01 per cent of the country's population lives in these districts. The average density of these districts is 6,888.[6]

The proportion of urban to total population has increased from 17.29 in 1951 to 25.72 in 1991. The total urban population in 1951 was estimated to be 62 million; this took a quantum jump to 218 million in 1991. By the turn of the century, the urban population is expected to be about one-third of the total population of the country.

Mumbai metropolis is the most populated city of the country with an urban population of 12.2 million, Calcutta taking the second place with 10.7 million. Delhi is third with an urban population of 8.2 million. Among the mega-cities of the world, Bombay comes at sixth place, Calcutta at ninth and Delhi at nineteenth. What is disturbing, however, is the annual average increase in the population of these cities: Bombay 416 thousand, Calcutta 171 thousand and Delhi 261 thousand. On the other hand, the corresponding figure for Tokyo, the most populous city of the world, is 316 thousand, for New York, the second most populous city, 46 thousand and Mexico, the third most populous city, 120 thousand. It would appear that the Indian urban agglomerations, particularly Bombay, would in the not too distant future overtake the other mega-cities. Many of India's cities are at very grave risk from both natural disasters and technological hazards. The concentration of population necessarily implies that the impact of disaster would, to that extent, be more devastating, affecting a much larger mass of humanity. As stated in the *World Disasters Report, 1998* "mega-cities of ten million or more people - sizes unprecedented historically - hold a daunting prospect for disaster prevention."[7]

The states of Tamilnadu and Kerala provide a silver lining with dramatic declines in birth rates. Their fertility rates are at, or close to, the levels in industrialized countries. But the fertility rate in Uttar Pradesh, Madhya Pradesh, Bihar and Rajasthan - the Hindi heartland - is about five children per couple, which is very much higher than the national average of 3.5. It is obvious that the country needs to have bold and imaginative strategies to bring down the current birth rate of 28 (per 1,000 of population) to about 20 in the next ten to fifteen years.

It has been said, though rather harshly, that "the increasing demographic load is bound to doom our coming generations (of Indians) either to a Malthusian nightmare or still worse to a Malthusian rot implying extreme poverty, starvation, unemployment, illiteracy, disease and violent conflicts - far worse than what we are facing now."[8] The following three vital areas would almost certainly be under enormous pressure:

- Agricultural production to feed the increasing numbers;
- Environment; and
- Quality of life of large sections of Indian people.

Uncontrolled population growth in India is not a mere demographic problem. It is an issue that will affect the economic well being of a big chunk of humanity and—what is even more significant and possibly sinister—it could disrupt their social fabric and even pose a threat to the democratic political structure.

INFRASTRUCTURE

India is an agricultural country. About half of the population is employed in the agriculture sector of the economy but this effort produces only about 20 per cent of the gross domestic product. Over the past 50 years since independence India has become one of the world's largest manufacturing countries. Economic reforms in the 1990s have encouraged privatization, attracted foreign investment, and facilitated the continued expansion of the country's infrastructure.

The existence of sound infrastructural facilities are essential not only for the economic development of a country but also to provide prompt relief in the event of disaster. The Government of India has been giving high priority to the development of infrastructural facilities. It has encouraged foreign investments in transport, communication and power sectors, and fiscal incentives have been offered to facilitate the flow of capital in these areas. The road sector has been declared an industry to facilitate borrowing on easy terms and to permit floating of bonds. The National Highways Act has been amended to enable levying of toll on national highways, bridges and tunnels. In the port sector, measures have been taken to encourage privatization. A new telecom policy has been announced which aims at upgrading the quality of telecom services to global standards. In the power sector, private participation is being promoted through measures like reduction of import duties, a five year tax holiday for new power projects and a 16 per cent return on equity.

Agriculture

The monsoon season determines the success or failure of agricultural production for the year. Too much rain brings flooding, structural damage–even disaster, affecting crops and livestock. Too little rain can bring drought and crop failure. In cyclone-prone areas of the country, crop and livestock losses result from storm-related flooding.

Much of India's agriculture depends on the July and August southwest monsoon, which decides the outcome for crops sown in June for harvest in October through January. In a similar way, India's southern peninsula depends upon the north-east monsoon. The Indian Government has placed a high priority on irrigation to reduce the vulnerability of farms to periods of drought, but the agriculture industry remains vulnerable to the vagaries of the monsoon season. Even now, about 40 percent of India's crops are rainfed.

Staple grains are wheat in northern India, and rice in the south and east. India has managed to bring food grain stocks to a high of 31.7 million tons (May 1994 figure). Current level of consumption is about one million tons per month, resulting in about a two-year supply for public distribution. Rice stocks tend to fall below target levels, and wheat stocks tends to be above desired levels. Complicating the issue of growing and producing food is the problematic issue of transportation and distribution during disaster incidents.[9] Efforts to modernize India's agricultural sector by means of irrigation, fertilisers, pesticides, and high-yield seeds has resulted in increased production, and India is now a net exporter of grains.

Transportation

Perhaps the most serious problem for providing disaster assistance during an emergency is the high vulnerability of transportation (and communications). Only 40 per cent of India's villages have all weather road connections, but seasonal flooding and rain can cause even surfaced roads to become impassable.[10]

India has nevertheless an elaborate transport system which plays an important role in the sustained economic growth of the country. It includes mainly the railways, roads, coastal shipping and air transport. The Ministry of Surface Transport formulates and implements policies and programs for the development of various modes of transport except the railways and the civil aviation for which there are separate ministries.

Railways

The railways have played a very vital role in the economic, industrial and social development of the country. From a very modest beginning in 1853, when the first train steamed off from Bombay to Thane, a distance of 34 kms, the Indian Railways have grown into a vast network of 7,068 stations spread over a route length of 62,915 kms. with a fleet of 6,909 locomotives, 33,450 passenger service vehicles, 5,654 other coaches and 2,80,791 wagons as on March 31, 1996.[11] It is, in fact, the principal mode of transportation today for passengers and freight.

About 20 per cent of the route kilometer, 28 per cent of running track kilometer and 27 per cent of total track kilometer is electrified. The network is divided into nine zones, which are further sub-divided into divisions. There are a total of about 1.6 million employees.

Train accidents in the country unfortunately occur with distressing frequency. The *Hindustan Times* recently listed the major train accidents (death toll exceeding 50) during the last ten years:[12]

July 8, 1988	107 people die as Island Express plunges into Ashtamudi Lake in Kerala
April 18, 1989	75 people killed as Karnataka Express derails near Lalitpur in U.P.
April 16, 1990	70 people burnt alive as a shuttle train catches fire near Patna
June 25, 1990	60 killed as a goods train rams into a passenger train near Mangra in Bihar

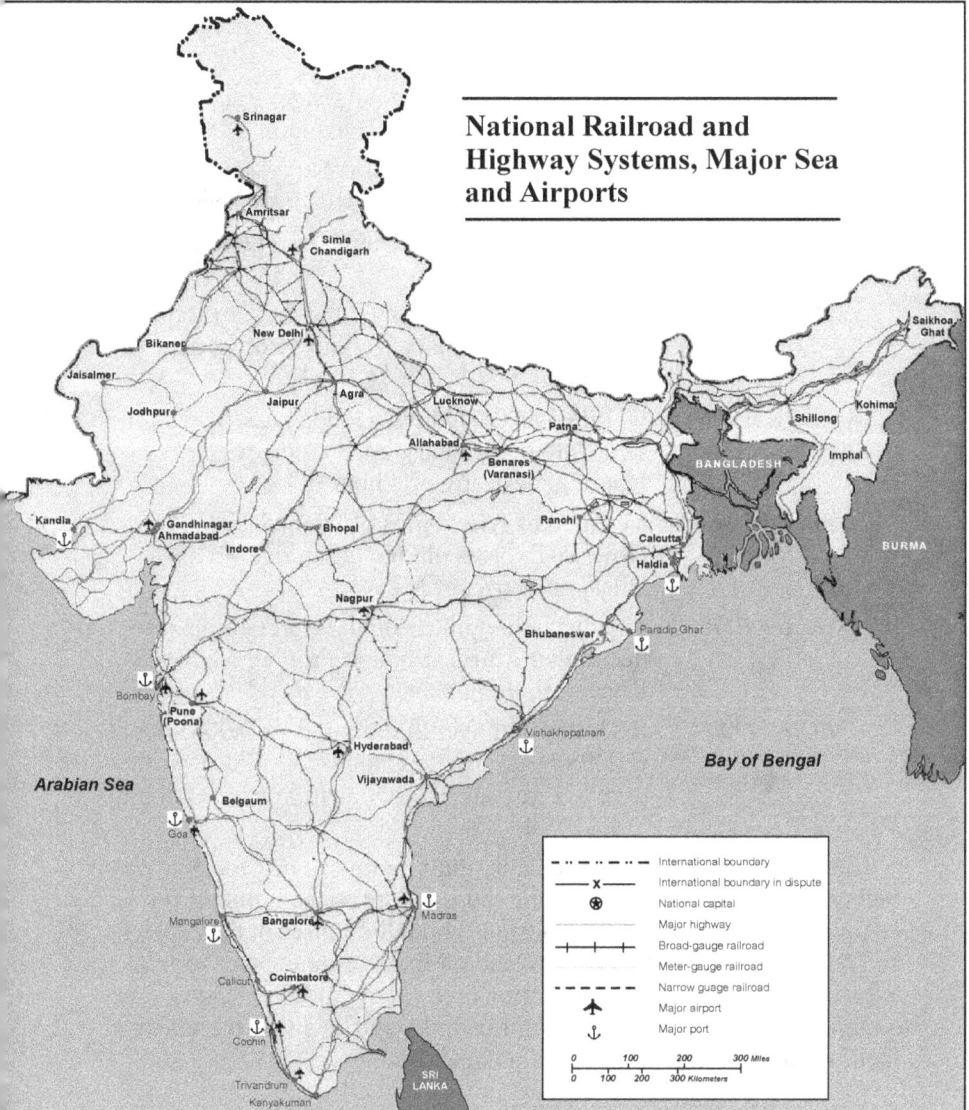

National Railroad and Highway Systems, Major Sea and Airports

Srinagar

Amritsar

Simla
Chandigarh

Bikaner

New Delhi

Saikhoa
Ghat

Jaisalmer

Jaipur   Agra

Lucknow

Kohima

Jodhpur

Allahabad

Patna

Shillong

Benares
(Varanasi)

BANGLADESH

Imphal

Kandla

Gandhinagar
Ahmadabad

Bhopal

Ranchi

Indore

Calcutta

Haldia

BURMA

Nagpur

Bhubaneswar

Paradip Ghar

Bombay

Pune
(Poona)

Hyderabad

Vishakhapatnam

Bay of Bengal

Arabian Sea

Belgaum

Vijayawada

Goa

Mangalore

Bangalore

Madras

Calicut

Coimbatore

Cochin

SRI
LANKA

Trivandrum

Kanyakumari

▬ ▪ ▬ ▪ ▬ ▪ ▬	International boundary
▬x▬	International boundary in dispute
⊛	National capital
	Major highway
╫╫╫╫	Broad-gauge railroad
	Meter-gauge railroad
▬ ▬ ▬	Narrow guage railroad
✈	Major airport
⚓	Major port

| 0 | 100 | 200 | 300 Miles |
| 0 | 100 | 200 | 300 Kilometers |

Figure III-5. National Railroad & Highway Systems, Major Sea and Air Ports.
Source: Based on Government of India map.

July 16, 1993	60 killed in mishap in Darbhanga district of Bihar
Sept. 21, 1993	71 killed as Kota-Bina passenger train rams into a goods train near Chhabra in Rajasthan
May 14, 1995	52 people killed as Madras-Kanyakumari Express collides with a goods train near Salem
June 1, 1995	73 killed in two accidents in West Bengal and Orissa
Aug 20, 1995	302 killed as Delhi-bound Purshottam Express rams into a stationary Kalindi Express near Firozabad in U.P.
April 18, 1996	60 killed as Gorakhpur-Gonda passenger train rams into a stationary goods train at Domingarh near Gorakhpur in UP
Sept 14, 1997	81 killed as five bogies of Ahmedabad Howrah-Express plunge into a river in Bilaspur district of MP
Nov 26, 1998	181 die as Jammu-Sealdah Express rams into decoupled Amritsar bound Frontier Mail near Khanna in Punjab
Jul 16, 1999	18 killed and over 200 injured as Delhi-bound G.T.Express from Chennai collides with derailed wagons of a goods train near Mathura.

Every time there is an accident, the Commissioner for Railway Safety is deputed to inquire into the causes of the mishap. But the public complain that they are rarely informed about the causes of the accident and responsibility for the same is seldom fixed. Maintenance of tracks is poor and the budgetary allocations for safety and maintenance are quite often sacrificed to sanction rail links and upgrade the existing facilities in politically favored constituencies.

Roads

India has the third largest road network in the world. The country's total road length was 30,15,229 kms in 1994-95. The Central Government's Eighth Plan laid emphasis on a coordinated and balanced development of road network which included: a primary road system covering the state highways; secondary and feeder road systems covering state highways and major district roads; and rural roads, including village roads and other district roads.[13]

The existing roads however do not facilitate speedy transportation due to the large proportion of unsurfaced roads (50 per cent) and the over-dependence on National Highways. The National Highways (38,445 kms.) account for less than 2 per cent of the total road length, though they carry as much as 40 per cent of the passengers and goods. Estimates indicate that by the year 2000 AD, road traffic will account for 85 per cent of passenger and 65 per cent of goods traffic. This calls for an urgent need to identify the major bottlenecks that impede the smooth flow of traffic and removing them.

The Government of India recently embarked on one of the biggest roads project ever undertaken in the country. The National Highways Road Development Project (NHRD) will connect Kashmir in the north of India to Kanyakumari at the southern-most tip of the peninsula; and it will connect Silchar in the north-east to Porbandar on the western coast. This 7,000 kilometer road project will cost Rs. 50 billion.

The absence of good roads, the rapid increase in the number of vehicular traffic in the wake of liberalization of the economy, and the variety of transportation using the same roads contribute to a large number of accidents and casualties.

The following chart gives the vehicular population, number of road accidents and casualties, their percentage variation over the previous year and the rate of accidental deaths (per thousand vehicles) during the last five years.

The number of motor vehicles in India increased by nearly 42 per cent during the period 1991-1995, and the number of road accidents

Year	Road Accidents (in 1,000)	% Variation Over Previous Year	Casualties in Road Accidents (in 1000)				Vehicle Population (in 100,000)	% Variation	Rate of Deaths (Per 1,000 vehicles)
			Persons Killed	% Varation over previous year	Persons Injured	% Varation over previous year			
1991	294	-----	56.6	-----	257.2	-----	213.74	-----	2.65
1992	259.3	-11.8	57.2	1.06	270	4.98	235.07	9.98	2.43
1993	279.3	7.71	60.6	5.94	289.7	7.3	255.05	8.5	2.38
1994	315.7	13.03	64.0	5.61	312.1	7.73	276.6	8.45	2.31
1995	328.1	3.93	59.9	-6.41	307.1	-1.6	302.87	9.5	1.98

FIG III-6. Accidental Deaths & Suicides in India, 1996.
Source: National Crime Records Bureau, Ministry of Home Affairs, Government of India.

55

during the same period increased by 11.6 percent. The rate of deaths per thousand vehicles decreased by nearly 25 per cent for the same period.

The Border Roads Development Board looks after the development of roads of strategic importance in the northern and north-eastern regions. It has so far constructed over 26,204 kms of roads and surfaced 27,925 kms of roads. The organization has now diversified to construction of airfields and buildings and permanent bridges involving high degree of technical expertise.

Waterways

India has about 15,655 kilometers of navigable waterways (rivers, canals, backwaters, creeks) for power driven boats and about 3,490 kilometers for large, commercial boats. Such travel is available principally on the Ganga and Brahmaputra rivers and tributaries, plus the Godavari, Mahanadi, Narmada, Tapti, and Krishna Rivers.[14] About 16 million tonnes of cargo is moved by Inland Water Transport. The Inland Waterways Authority (IWT) of India is entrusted with the responsibility of development, maintenance and regulation of national waterways and also to advise the Central and the State governments on matters relating to the development of IWT. The government has identified ten important waterways with a view to declaring them as National Waterways.

Shipping and Ports

The country has the largest merchant shipping fleet among developing countries and ranks 17th in the world in shipping tonnage. As on December 31, 1996, the net operative tonnage consisted of 484 ships totalling 70,51,546 GRT. There are about 84 shipping companies in the country. The National Shipping Board advises the Central Government on shipping matters.

India has 11 major ports which handle around 90 per cent of the sea borne trade. These are managed by Port Trusts under the Central Government. In addition, there are 139 minor / intermediate ports which are under the State Governments. During 1996-97, the total cargo handled at major ports was 227.3 million tonnes.

Kandla, Gujarat State; Mumbai, Maharastra State; Mormugao, Goa State; New Mangalore, Karnataka State; Cochin, Kerala State; and Jawaharlal Nehru Port are the major ports along the west coast. The major ports on the east coast are Tuticorin and Chennai of Tamil Nadu

State; Visakhapatnam of Andhra Pradesh State; Paradip, Orissa State; and Calcutta-Haldia, West Bengal State.[15]

A major problem with the ports is the mismatch between the existing capacity and the demand for traffic. As against the total capacity of 217.3 million tonnes on March 31, 1997, the major ports handled 227.3 million tonnes in 1996-97, resulting in pre-berthing delays and longer ship turn-around time. The capacity needs to be augmented keeping in view the projected traffic requirements.

The government is encouraging private investment in the port sector. The first large private project in the port sector has been taken up at the Jawaharlal Nehru Port, Navi Mumbai for construction, management and maintenance of a Two Berth Container Terminal for a 30 year period by an Australia led consortium. Similarly, license has been awarded to the Port of Singapore Authority (PSA) for the development of a container terminal on BOT basis for a 30 year period. The state governments of Gujarat, Maharashtra and Andhra Pradesh have embarked on ambitious port development programs through private participation. A Maritime States Development Council (MSDC) has been formed to ensure an integrated approach to the development of both major and minor ports.

Civil Aviation

The civil aviation sector has the Indian Airlines, Alliance Air (a subsidiary of Indian Airlines) and private scheduled airlines and air taxis which cater to the domestic air services. The Indian Airlines' operations extend to the neighboring countries of South-East Asia and Middle East also. The Air India takes care of the international air services. The Department of Civil Aviation formulates the national policies and programs for the development and regulation of civil aviation and for devising and implementing schemes for the growth and expansion of civil air transport. Its functions also extend to overseeing the provision of airport facilities, air traffic services and carriage of passengers and goods by air.

The Directorate General of Civil Aviation (DGCA) is the regulatory organization for enforcing civil air regulations. The Bureau of Civil Aviation Security (BCAS) is the nodal body for all civil aviation security matters.

The Airports Authority of India was formed in 1995 by merger of the International Airports Authority of India and the National Airports Authority. The main functions of the Authority are to provide safe and efficient Air Traffic Services, Communication and Navigational Aids at all the airports; plan, develop, construct and maintain runways, taxi-ways, apron, terminal buildings, etc.; provide Air Safety Services; and Search and Rescue facilities in coordination with other agencies.[16]

Communication

Mass communications are essential to warn, prepare and equip people in the face of any disaster. Radio and television have both a comprehensive reach throughout the length and breadth of the country.

The All India Radio Air is a national service that is operated by the Ministry of Information and Broadcasting of the Government of India. AIR network has 198 broadcasting centers. The AIR has a total of 303 transmitters: these include 144 medium-wave, 55 short-wave and 103 FM transmitters. They provide radio coverage to 97.3 per cent of the population and their signals spread over 90 per cent area of the country.[17]

Doordarshan is the national television service of India and it is one of the largest broadcasting organizations in the world. It covers 87.6 per cent of the population operating from 47 studios on 20 channels. Channel DD-1 provides national, regional and local programming; DD-2 is an entertainment channel that uses terrestrial transmitters in 47 cities; DD-4 through 13 are regional language channels; DD-14 through 17 are Hindi speaking channels; DD-18 is the Punjabi regional service. DD-India provides international service, DD-Sports is a sports channel, and DD-News offers news and current affairs. The TV audience in India includes some 65 million homes (14 million homes have cable TV). Doordarshan claims to reach 362 million people on DD-1 and 138 million on DD-2.[18]

The country has a telecommunication network of over 22,530 telephone exchanges with a capacity of 18.91 million lines and 15.85 million working connections (as on December 31 1997). These exchanges are linked with 30,968 route km. of co-axial cable, 54,597 M/w route km. of microwave systems, 62,670 route km of UHF systems and 52,432 route km. of the latest state-of-art optical fibre systems. The country's remote areas are linked to the network through 209 satellite earth stations. All the district headquarters have STD (subscriber trunk dialling) facility. Satellite based remote Area Business Message Network, a new technology, is under operation for exchange of data facsimile, telex messages, etc. 586 VSATs (Very Small Aperture Terminals) are in operation.[19]

The expansion of the telecom sector is being carried out under the National Telecom Policy (NTP) which *inter alia* lays down that every village is to be provided with at least one public telephone. The work has been entrusted to the Department of Telecommunications (DOT) as well as to licensed private companies. Out of 6,04,374 villages in the country, 2,67,832 villages were provided with telephones till the end of March 1997. Foreign investors desirous of investing in the manufacture of telecom equipment are allowed automatic approval upto 51 per cent of foreign equity. The telecom equipment manufacturing industry has been delicensed and dereserved.

A number of services have been franchised to private/public Indian registered companies on a non-exclusive basis. These include Cellular Mobile Telephone Service, Radio Paging Service, Electronic Mail, Voice-Mail, Video-Conferencing etc. There were about 150 thousand subscribers of Cellular Mobile Telephone Service as on September 30, 1997. India's Department of Telecommunications and Videsh Sanchar Nigam Limited (VSNL) are now working to expand the Internet services.

Power

Power supplies have not kept pace with the demand, but a government policy of liberalization and allowing private and foreign companies to participate in the industry has improved the situation. There is a strong emphasis on rural electrification. About 90,000 of some 600,000 villages are without electric power and about the same number have a very limited availability of power.[20]

Power generation in 1996-97 was 394.5 billion kwh, indicating a growth of 3.8 per cent over 1995-96. The total generation of power during April - February 1997-98 was 382.8 billion kwh, higher than 358.7 billion kwh achieved during April - February 1996-97, recording a growth of 6.7 per cent. Hydro generation grew by 6.2 per cent , thermal by 6.7 per cent, and nuclear generation by 13.4 per cent. The low Plant Load Factor (PLF) of thermal plants, heavy transmission and distribution losses suffered by the State Electricity Boards (SEBs) and other operational and technical inefficiencies led to constrained utilization of the existing capacities.[21]

The thermal plants presently account for 73 per cent of the total power generation; hydro-electric plants contribute 25 per cent and the nuclear plants only 2 per cent.[22] The non-official estimate of India's installed capacity of power generation (public utilities), as of 1997, was 96.1 MW.[23]

The Power Grid Corporation of India Limited has been entrusted with the responsibility of setting up a National Power Grid which would comprise strong regional networks with suitable synchronous High Voltage Direct Current links between the regions. There are five regional grid systems, namely, northern, western, southern, eastern and north-eastern covering all the states of the country.

The central participation in the expansion of power generation program started in 1975 with the creation of two generating corporations, namely, National Thermal Power Corporation (NTPC) and the National Hydro Power Corporation (NHPC), which gave fillip to the growth of the power sector in the country.

The NTPC has an installed capacity of 16,795 MW, representing about 28 per cent of the all India thermal capacity. The Corporation has successfully commissioned super thermal power projects at Singrauli (UP), Korba (MP), Ramagundam (AP), Farakka (WB), Vindhyachal (MP), Rihand (UP), Dadri (UP), Kahalgaon (Bihar), Talcher (Orissa) and five combined cycle gas power projects at Anta (Rajasthan), Auraiya (UP), Dadri (UP), Kawas (Gujarat) and Gandhar (Gujarat). The NHPC has so far completed construction of seven hydro-electric projects at Baira Siul (Himachal Pradesh), Loktak (Manipur), Salal (J&K), Tanakpur (UP), Chamera (MP) and Uri (J&K). These power stations have a total installed capacity of 2133 MW.

The Government of India has drawn up an ambitious plan called Power Vision India-2010, envisaging capacity addition of 80,000 MW in the next twelve years. It has also set up four task forces with regard to hydro, thermal, system improvements and power projects to ensure timely completion of the identified projects.

Nuclear Power and Nuclear Weapons

India has presently five nuclear power stations consisting of ten reactors and ten turbo alternates located at five sites. Besides, work on the two units at Kaiga (Karnataka) and units 3 and 4 of the Rajasthan Atomic Power Project are in progress. Out of these 14 units, the only reactors which use enriched Uranium are those at Tarapur.

The Kalpakkam Reprocessing Plant (KARP) was recently, on Sept.15, 1998, dedicated to the nation. With its commissioning, India can reprocess spent fuel for fast breeder reactors. Dr. R.Chidambaram, Chairman, Atomic Energy Commission, announced on the occasion that India's target was to produce 20,000 MW of nuclear power by 2020 AD.

The nuclear power plants in India have adopted a defense in depth approach for the design of reactors.[24] These addresss issues of fuel, construction and safety:

- *Fuel:* Use of natural or low enriched Uranium which ensures that the total fissile material available in the core is much below that required to form a critical mass which might cause an explosion and damage the containment.

- *Cladding:* The Zircalloy cladding, in which the ceramic fuel is located, is capable of withstanding temperatures that obtain at the center of Uranium fuel during the operation.

- *Leak Tight Heat Transport System:* The Zircalloy fuel tubes containing Uranium-235 are enveloped in Primary Heat Transport System piping and tubes which is designed for a pressure of 103.9 kg/sq.cm. against the designed system operating pressure of 87 kg/sq.cm.

- *Containment* : All the nuclear power plants are designed to hold the radioactive material from their reactor cores within their containment.

- *Exclusion Zone* : There is an exclusion zone of 1.6 km. around the plant which is fenced to prevent any unauthorized entry or habitation within the zone. The limit is reduced to 0.8 km. in case of stations which have full double containments.

Fuel reprocessing and nuclear waste management constitute the back end of the nuclear power program. As a result of the research and development carried out at the Bhaba Atomic Research Center (BARC), these technologies are now established in the country. The waste treatment, conditioning and disposal systems are operating at nuclear installations. At Tarapur, a waste immobilization plant is operational and an interim storage facility has also been set up. A program of siting a repository in suitable deep geological formations for final disposal of immobilized high level radioactive wastes is also in progress.

- *Nuclear Weapons:* The demonstration of its nuclear weapons capability by India in the summer of 1998, placed India openly within the military "nuclear club" of countries and raised concerns about the possibility of a nuclear disaster in the Indian subcontinent. India's geostrategic location amidst potential belligerant countries suggests that disaster managment and civil defense professionals must account for the possiblity of nuclear accidents–indeed, acts of war–in disaster planning.

It may be recalled that there was a military confrontation between India and China in 1962 in which India suffered a humiliating defeat. In the following years, however, there was a conscious effort by both the countries to mend the fences. The Deng Xiaoping formula of keeping the sensitive border dispute on hold and move towards confidence building measures on other fronts seemed to be working. Relations were gradually improving - until India's Defense Minister's statement that China was India's potential "threat number 1." The nuclear explosions by India and the announcement that Indian scientists had been given the clearance to develop an improved version of the Agni ICBM sent alarm bells ringing in Beijing. The Chinese leaders also raised the ante and have been accusing India of escalating tension in South Asia.

A number of contentious issues remain unresolved between India and China. These are the Sino-Pakistan missile and nuclear collaboration, China claiming Arunachal Pradesh as part of its territory and holding on to Aksai Chin in the Ladakh area, incidents of Chinese incursions, and the issue of Line of Actual Control.

The Indo-Pakistan confrontation over Kashmir, however, poses the more proximate threat to peace and stability in the sub-continent. There were wars between the two countries in 1947, 1965 and 1971. With the acquisition of nuclear capability by both India and Pakistan, the temperature is approaching a flash-point. The problem remains unresolved, in part because of Pakistan's continued sponsorship of Islamic terrorism and subversion which impacts upon the Kashmir situation. Additionally, Indians are concerned that a nuclear first strike could be a key part of Pakistani military strategy, while they believe that India's nuclear weapons represent a deterrent of last resort.

The dimensions and the magnitude of disaster in the event of nuclear confrontation between India and Pakistan would be horrendous. It will be a "scary scenario" observed Col. Mike Pasquarett, Director of Operations and Gaming at the US Army War College's Center for Strategic Leadership, which ran a war game involving the Indian subcontinent.[25] *Outlook*, an important weekly newsmagazine of India, has drawn a lurid picture of the scenario.[26] It says that a 1 megaton thermo-nuclear device dropped by an F16 in Delhi would mean that 9,000,000 people shall perish or, in other words, only one out of ten persons would have the chance of survival. Everyone within a seven km radius will be killed instantly. A similar strike in Bombay would wipe out around 8,936,000 people. Delhi and Bombay would be likely targets because a very high percentage of national wealth is concentrated in these metropolitan centers. It is also apprehended that Pakistan shall focus on energy and transport targets like the atomic power plants at Tarapur (near Bombay), Kakrapar (in Gujarat), Kota (in Rajasthan) and Narora (in UP).

The American *Newsweek* has also painted a horrific picture of the impact of a nuclear exchange between the sub-continental neighbors. It states that in a full-scale "city-busting" exchange, more than 17 million Pakistani and 29 million Indians would die within the first few hours. The medical services would be overwhelmed with Pakistan having just 59 hospital beds and 48 physicians per 100,000 of population and India having 74 beds and 47 physicians per 100,000 of population. The total number of dead, according to a 1992 study sponsored by the US Air Force, could reach 100 million. Besides, depending on the season, "the blasts could coat a huge region - from China to Southeast Asia - with fallout."[27] It is difficult to expect that disaster management professionals will be able to comprehend, indeed effectively plan for, the consequences of such a disaster.

Water and Dams

Schemes for the supply of drinking water in rural areas are formulated and implemented by the States under the Minimum Needs Program (MNP). Central assistance is provided under the Accelerated Rural Water Supply Program with 100 per cent grants-in-aid to a matching provision made by the State Governments under the MNP. Currently (March 1997), about 86 per cent of people in urban and rural areas have drinking water facilities.[28]

Rapid urbanization and industrialization are increasing the challenge of providing basic amenities to the people. The Accelerated Urban Water Supply Program is aimed at providing safe and adequate drinking water to the entire population of towns having less than 20,000 people (as per 1991 census) in the country. As on December 31, 1997, water supply schemes had been approved for 254 towns in various States which account for only 11.8 per cent of the total number of such towns.

According to *People's Science Institute*, an NGO, the government's water management policies have been a failure.[29] The fundamental reason for this lies in the nature of the development planning model that India has adopted, emphasizing the maximization of certain benefits, usually for the well-to-do classes, at the expense of the environment - and hence the rural poor. Besides, the environmental and social costs are usually ignored in the cost-benefit estimates of big dam projects. The other fundamental flaw is the engineering approach with its focus on big dams. Very little attention is paid to the use of soil moisture, where most of the rainwater is usually trapped. The focus of planning, the Institute says, should shift to rainfed lands and to crop management as part of a rational water policy. Enhancing the productivities of these lands would be essential to meet India's food requirements in the next century.

A recent John Hopkins Population Information report visualises that by the year 2025 AD, population will push India and 16 other countries into the list of nations facing water crisis and water scarcity. The study reminds that there is no more fresh water on earth than there was 2,000 years ago, when the population was three per cent of its current size.[30] The report says that nearly half-a-billion people around the world face water shortage today. By 2025 AD, the number will explode five-fold to 2.8 billion people - 35 per cent of the world's projected total of eight billion people.

Sharing of river waters between the states is already creating major problems. There was a prolonged dispute spread over seven years between the Cauvery Basin states of Tamilnadu, Karnataka, Kerala and Pondicherry over sharing the waters of Cauvery river. The Supreme Court had to intervene in the matter and eventually the Government of India notified, on August 11, 1998, the setting up a Cauvery River Authority with Prime Minister as the chairperson and the chief ministers of Tamilnadu, Karnataka, Kerala and Pondicherry as its members, and a Monitoring Committee comprising officials. The Authority would implement the 1991 interim order of the Cauvery Water Disputes Tribunal which had laid down that Karnataka should release water from its reservoirs to ensure that 205 TMCFt (thousand million cubic feet) of water was available in Tamilnadu's Metttur reservoir (in a water year) from June to May.

Dams in India have been built with the objectives of flood control or for providing irrigation and power benefits. The Hirakud and the Damodar Valley Corporation (DVC) were built essentially to store the flood waters. The Bhakra reservoir was conceived and built primarily for providing irrigation and power benefits. The areas protected by structural measures however experience drainage congestion during floods in the rivers, particularly in the flood plains. Some experts favor living with the floods and depending on non-structural flood management measures such as flood forecasting, flood warning, flood preparedness, flood plain zoning, flood proofing, flood fighting and flood relief. The Eighth Plan actually accorded greater thrust to non-structural measures of flood management.

The *People's Science Institute* is of the view that big dams have not given the benefits that were expected of them due to the following reasons:[31]

- The planning and design of dams is based on poor data. Basic design parameters, e.g., siltation rates, water flows, submergence areas, etc. were incorrectly determined.

- The project design and execution emphasis are usually lopsided as they concentrate mainly on the construction of the dam and less on the water delivery systems.

- Some dams are located in seismic regions, posing the threat of reservoir-induced earthquakes - as happened at Koyna and is now perceived in Tehri.

- A powerful lobby of engineers, construction companies, politicians, bureaucrats and farmers in the command areas have often pushed for mega projects in their own self interest at the cost of powerless and the environment.

Medha Patkar, chairperson of the *Narmada Bachao Andolan*, has been vigorously campaigning against the raising of any new dams for these reasons. The multi-crore Narmada Dam Project has been stalled mainly because of her unrelenting opposition to it. The Supreme Court has stayed any further construction on the project till the issues relating to the rehabilitation of all those who are going to be displaced are settled.

Most damage to the infrastructure sectors described above is caused by floods, but earthquakes, winds, landslides, and other hazards take their toll also. In the following chapter, the authors discuss the services that compliment India's infrastructure.

Endnotes

1. As quoted by Jyotshna Pandit "Why do floods wreak havoc?" *Daily Excelsior*(Jammu (Jammu & Kashmir), India), 19 September 1999, available from <http://www.dailyexcelsior.com/99sep19/edit.htm#7>, Internet; accessed 22 February 2000.

2. D. M. Silveira, *India Book 1998-99* (Bombay: Classic Publishers), 88.

3. Ministry of Health and Family Welfare, *Annual Report 1997-1998* (New Delhi: Government of India, 1997),1.

4. Statistical Outline of India, 1997-98 (Mumbai: Tata Donnelley Ltd., December 1997), 37; also Statistical Abstract India 1997 (New Delhi: Central Statistical Organization, December 1997), 29.

5. Ministry of Health and Family Welfare, 3.

6. Ministry of Information and Broadcasting, India 1998: A Reference Manual (New Delhi: Government of India: 1998), 6.

7. International Federation of Red Cross and Red Crescent Societies, World Disasters Report 1998 (Oxford, U.K.: Oxford University Press), 12-15.

8. K.B.Sahay, *Heading for Disaster* (Times of India, July 4, 1997).

9. "Disaster Relief Plan," U.S. Mission to India (New Delhi: U.S. AID, 9 March 1998), 16.

10. "Disaster Relief Plan," 13.

11. Ministry of Information and Broadcasting, 701.

12. S. S. Banyal, "Another Mishap, but Will the Public Know Why?" *Hindustan Times* (27 November 1998).

13. Ibid., 469.

14. "Inland Waterways," India Country Study (Quantico: USMC, 1997); available from <India Handbook/India_Sect12.html>, Internet; accessed 3 December 97.

15. D. M. Silveira, *India Book 1998-99*(Bombay: Classic Publishers, 1998), 84.

16. Ministry of Information and Broadcasting, 479.

17. All India Radio, available from <www.air.kode.net>, Internet; accessed 12 February 2000.

18. Doordarshan, Indian National Television Network; available from <www.ddindia.net>, Internet: accessed 12 February 2000.

19. Ministry of Finance, Economic Division, *Economic Survey, 1997-1998* (New Delhi: Government of India, 1998), 128.

20. "Disaster Relief Plan," 15.

21. Ibid., 125.

22.*Statistical Abstract India 1997* , Central Statistical Organisation, Department of Statistics, Ministry of Planning and Programme Inplementation (New Delhi: Government of India, December, 1997), 170.

23.*Statistical Outline of India* , *1997-98*, 69.

24. P. C. Sinha, ed., *Encyclopaedia of Disaster Management*, Vol 10, *Technological Disasters* (New Delhi: Anmol Publications, 1998), 280-1.

25. Thomas E. Ricks, "War Games Fuel U.S. Military's Fear of South Asian Rivalry," *The Indian Express*(New Delhi), 25 June 1998.

26.*Outlook* , 25 May 1998.

27.*Newsweek* , 8 June 1998.

28.*Ministry* of Finance,149.

29. People's Science Institute, Ravi Chopra, Director, *Water and People: A National Perspective, 1998*(Dehra Doon, India: 1998),

11. (PSI is a nonprofit, public interest research organization. Its main function is to provide technical support services to social action groups. The two major disciplines at PSI are water resources management and environmental quality monitoring. In water resources management, PSI works on problems with flood control, droughts, irrigation and watershed development.)

30. *Hindustan Times*, September 4 1998.

31. People's Science Institute, 12-13.

IV. Services

*With its vast territory, large population and unique geo-climatic
conditions, the Indian sub-continent is exposed to natural
catastrophes traditionally.[1]*

Vulnerability Atlas of India

Complementing India's physical infrastructure are the
government services available to protect lives and property
during disaster incidents. Private organizations also contribute
significant support to the Indian people, and these organizations are
addressed in the following chapter. This chapter briefly outlines the
scope and capacity of medical, fire, civil defense, home guards, police,
paramilitary, and defense forces that can be made available to battle the
consequences of a disaster.

MEDICAL AND PUBLIC HEALTH

Public health, sanitation and hospitals are a State responsibility in
India. Some charitable, voluntary and private institutions also provide
medical relief. India's Central Government establishes health policy
and provides funding to the states. Within the states, the district and
sub-divisional hospitals serve as the primary health care centers.

Drugs used are mostly manufactured in India by the government and
private companies. Because of the shortage of electricity in rural areas,
cold storage for drugs is often unavailable there, but refrigeration is
available in the urban areas. The government's Medical Stores
Organization has depots in Bombay, Madras, Calcutta, Karnal,
Hyderabad, and Guwahati. These depots maintain civil defense stocks
and mobile hospital units for emergency use.[2]

The latest available figures of medical facilities which serve the
country's nearly one billion people are as follows:[3]

Doctors	489,189
Medical Colleges	162
Annual Out-turn of Doctors	17,000
Dental Surgeons	113,000
Nurses	559,896
Hospitals	13,692

71

Dispensaries	28,321
Beds	596,203
Beds per 100,000 population	70

Although health is a state subject under the Constitution, the Central Government's intervention is needed in the areas of control and eradication of major communicable and non-communicable diseases, broad policy formulation, international health, medical and para-medical education. It also oversees drug control, prevention of food adulteration, and activities concerning the population including safe motherhood, child survival and immunization programs.

The major health schemes for control and eradication of communicable diseases include the National Programs for Eradication of Malaria, Leprosy, Tuberculosis and AIDS (including Blood Safety Measures and STD Control). The National Programs for control of non-communicable diseases like Cancer, Cataract Blindness, Iodine Deficiency Disorders and Mental Health are also being implemented.

The Directorate General of Health Services, Ministry of Health & Family Welfare, Government of India provides technical assistance to the states to improve the health sector response. The responsibility is discharged by the Emergency Medical Relief Division of the Directorate General of Health Services.

As in other countries, India has taken steps to educate medical professionals about their role in the organization and processes of disaster relief. The following training activities were conducted under the WHO funded program by the disaster management collaborating centers with a view to creating awareness among the officials of the health and other departments on various aspects of health sector disaster management.[4]

- Jawahar Lal Institute of Post-Graduate Medical Education and Research (JIPMER), Pondicherry: Organized activities on Hospital Contingency Plan.

- National Institute of Communicable Diseases, Delhi: Organized a training course for medical officers on disaster management with special reference to epidemic preparedness and response.

- All India Institute of Hygiene and Public Health, Calcutta: Organized a training program on health sector preparedness for North-Eastern States and for elected leaders of West Bengal.

- Central Health Education Bureau (CHEB), New Delhi: Involved in preparation of Information, Education and Communication material related to disaster management.

- Administrative Staff College of India, Hyderabad: Imparted training on management aspects of disaster preparedness.

- Sardar Patel Institute of Public Administration, Ahmedabad: Organized three workshops / training activities on disaster management during 1997.

- National Environmental Engineering and Research Institute, Nagpur: Conducting research on methodologies of health risk assessment during disasters. A workshop on emergency preparedness and response to chemical hazards was organized.

The above programs have contributed to building up a cadre of officials in the health and other departments who are sensitive to natural calamities and are conversant with the drill to be adopted and the procedures to be followed in the event of a disaster so as to provide necessary relief to the affected population.

FIRE FIGHTING

The fire services in the country are administered by the States and Union Territories as fire is a state subject. The Ministry of Home Affairs renders technical advice to States and Union Territories and the Central ministries on fire protection, fire prevention and fire legislation. The National Fire Service College, Nagpur, conducts different types of courses for the training of fire officers in India; it is the only college of its kind in South-East Asia and it trains fire officers of several countries. The College had, till March 1997, trained 11,000 fire officers including 100 foreign trainees in different courses. There were, till mid-1997, a total of 2,023 fire stations operating in the country manned by 64,048 fire professionals with a fleet of 6,202 appliances/vehicles of various specifications.

CIVIL DEFENSE

Civil Defense aims at saving life, minimizing damage to property and maintaining continuity of industrial production in the event of a hostile attack. The Director General of Civil Defense (usually a police officer) works under the Ministry of Home Affairs. Each state and territory has a Director of Civil Defense who works under the Home

Department. Central financial assistance to the states for Civil Defense measures is confined to categorized towns only. Civil Defense is primarily organized on a voluntary basis except for a small nucleus of paid staff and establishment which is augmented during emergencies. The Civil Defense activities presently extend to 162 towns spread over 32 States and Union Territories. The target is to have 815,000 Civil Defense volunteers, the current strength being 452,000.[5]

The National Civil Defense College, Nagpur, a subordinate training establishment of the Ministry of Home Affairs, conducts various courses in Civil Defense and Disaster Relief Management. The College has, since its inception in 1957, trained 29,000 personnel. The Civil Defense volunteers are extensively deployed in relief and rescue work during disasters such as earthquakes and cyclones.

HOME GUARDS

The Home Guards originated from state-level voluntary citizens' forces organized in 1946 to support the police and their functions. After the conflict with China in 1962, these forces were consolidated as Home Guards under Union direction. They are a police auxiliary and they also support local government during emergencies such as fires, cyclones, earthquakes and the like. They also participate in socio-economic and welfare activities.[6]

In the border states, Border Wing Home Guards Battalions have also been raised, which serve as an auxiliary to the security forces. The total authorized strength of the Home Guards in the country is 573,793 against which the raised strength is 450,000 Home Guards. The organization is spread over all the States and Union Territories except in Kerala and Arunachal Pradesh.[7]

All citizens of the country in the age group of 18-50 are eligible to become members of Home Guards. The normal tenure of membership in Home Guards is three to five years. A Home Guard, whenever called for duty or training, is paid duty or training allowance at prescribed rates to meet out-of-pocket expenses. Home Guards with three years of service in the organization and trained in the basic and refresher courses are given preference in recruitment to some basic posts in the Central Government as well as in the state government services.

The Ministry of Home Affairs formulates the policy in respect of the role, raising, training, equipping, establishment and other important matters of the Home Guards. Expenditure on Home Guards is shared between the Union and the State Governments.

74

POLICE

The police is entrusted with the responsibility of preventing and detecting crime and maintaining law and order. Public order being a state subject under the Constitution, police is maintained and controlled by the states.

The police organization is headed by a Director General of Police at the state level. He is assisted by Inspectors General of Police who look after police matters at the zonal level, the state being divided into several zones. The zones are further split into ranges which are commanded by Deputy Inspectors General of Police. A range comprises three to five districts. At the district level, which is the basic unit of administration, the police force is headed by a Superintendent of Police. The police have specialized wings for criminal investigation of cases of a serious nature, economic offenses, intelligence matters, as well as armed battalions.

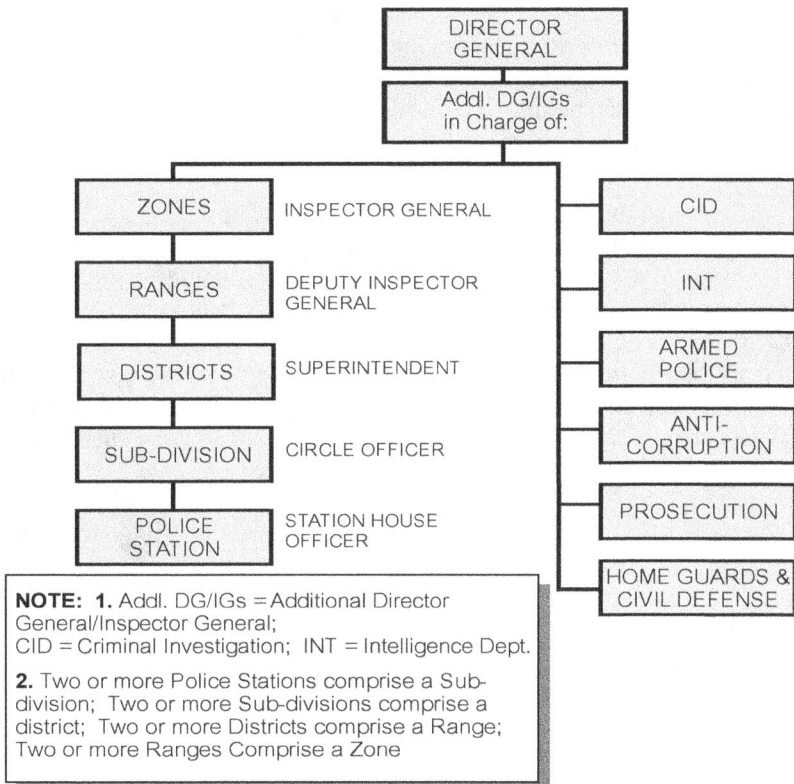

Figure IV-1, **State Police Organizaton.** Source: Authors.

The Indian Police is modeled on a legislative enactment of 1861. The British had designed the Act to subserve their imperial interests and ensure that the police acted under all circumstances as an agent of the executive. It is unfortunate that even after independence a new legislation has not been enacted so far, possibly because the successive governments found it convenient to use and misuse the police for their partisan ends. Several State Police Commissions and the National Police Commission recommended sweeping reforms in the organization, structure and accountability of the police, but these have not been carried out. As a result, the hiatus between the police and the general mass of people has continued to grow. There are credible complaints of corruption, inefficiency and human rights violations against the police.

The Supreme Court of India has taken cognizance of a public interest petition for implementation of the National Police Commission recommendations. There are hopeful signs that judicial intervention would compel the government to introduce the long-delayed reforms. The police is presently accountable to the executive; this is likely to change and the police would perhaps in the near future be made accountable to the people of the country and the laws of the land. Once this fundamental change is brought about, the police response to disaster situations would also show substantial improvement.

The police functions cover a very wide spectrum. There is hardly a sphere of activity where the police is not called upon to play a role. In fact, most of the other government organizations including the Excise, Transport and Income Tax depend heavily on police for the performance of their duties. In times of disaster, natural or man made, the police is generally the first to react and take action for the regulation and diversion of traffic, removal of debris and evacuation of casualties. The enormous manpower of the police and its resources enable it to provide the first healing touch in any emergency.

The all India strength of the police force, as on January 1, 1998, was 1,374,608.[8] Besides, every state has armed police battalions, the total strength of such battalions in the country being 283. The largest police force is of the State of Uttar Pradesh, which has a total strength of 169,000 including 34 battalions of the armed police. In terms of population, there are 14.34 policemen per 10,000 of population. In terms of area, 42.54 policemen look after an area of 100 sq. kms. Considering the population of the country, the police strength is inadequate.

PARAMILITARY FORCES

The Government of India has a large paramilitary force structure which is employed to assist the states in their responsibility to maintain public order. Five Central Paramilitary Forces are under the direction of the Home Secretary: Border Security Force (BSF); Central Reserve Police Force (CRPF); Indo-Tibetan Border Police (ITBP); Central Industrial Security Force (CISF); and National Security Guard (NSG). The Assam Rifles (AR), on the other hand, is under the Ministry of Defense. Each of these forces has a well defined role.[9]

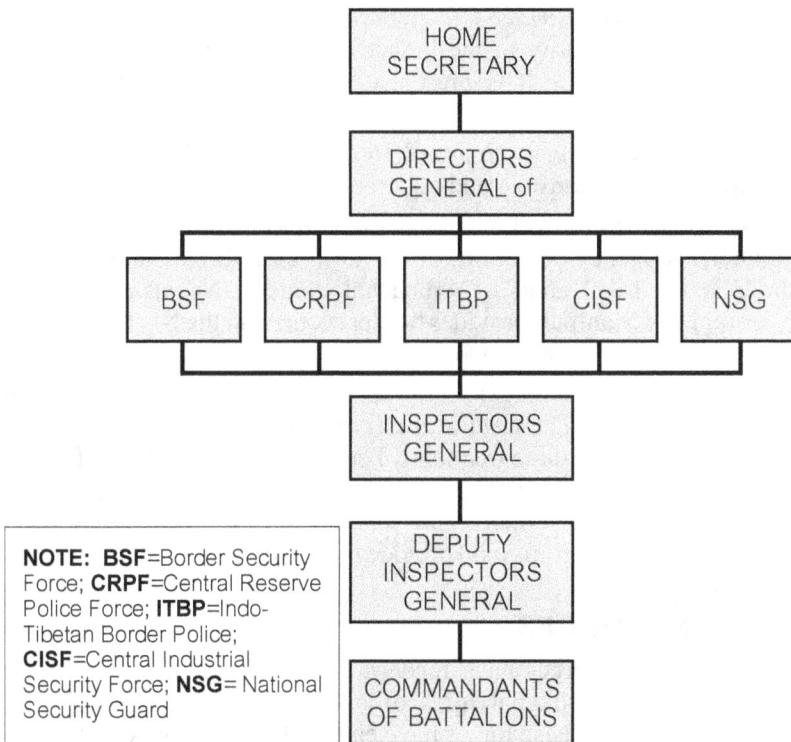

```
                    ┌──────────────────┐
                    │      HOME        │
                    │    SECRETARY     │
                    └──────────────────┘
                    ┌──────────────────┐
                    │    DIRECTORS     │
                    │   GENERAL of     │
                    └──────────────────┘
   ┌───────┬───────────┬───────────┬───────────┬───────┐
┌──────┐ ┌──────┐  ┌──────┐   ┌──────┐   ┌──────┐
│ BSF  │ │ CRPF │  │ ITBP │   │ CISF │   │ NSG  │
└──────┘ └──────┘  └──────┘   └──────┘   └──────┘
                    ┌──────────────────┐
                    │   INSPECTORS     │
                    │    GENERAL       │
                    └──────────────────┘
                    ┌──────────────────┐
                    │     DEPUTY       │
                    │   INSPECTORS     │
                    │    GENERAL       │
                    └──────────────────┘
                    ┌──────────────────┐
                    │  COMMANDANTS     │
                    │ OF BATTALIONS    │
                    └──────────────────┘
```

NOTE: **BSF**=Border Security Force; **CRPF**=Central Reserve Police Force; **ITBP**=Indo-Tibetan Border Police; **CISF**=Central Industrial Security Force; **NSG**= National Security Guard

Figure IV-2, **Central Paramilitary Forces.** Source: Authors.

The Border Security Force (185,000, 156 battalions) is essentially for deployment along the international borders to prevent trans-border crimes, unauthorized entry into or exit from the territory of India, and to prevent smuggling and any other illegal activity.

77

The Central Reserve Police Force (165,300, 135 battalions) is the premier internal security force of the Central Government, and it assists the states in handling major law and order situations. It has an elite unit known as the Rapid Action Force, which was raised in 1992, to deal with communal riots and riot-like situations.

The Indo-Tibetan Border Police (32,200; 29 battalions) is to keep vigil along the border with Tibet. Its personnel are deployed at altitudes ranging from 9,000 to 18,000 feet above the sea level along the border with Tibet , which extends from Karakoram pass in Ladakh to Lipu lake pass at the tri-junction of Indo-Tibet-Nepal border.

The Central Industrial Security Force   (88,600) is to provide protection and security to the industrial undertakings owned by the central government. It is presently inducted in 233 public sector undertakings.

The National Security Guard (7,360) is an elite commando force to be utilized in anti-terrorist and counter-hijacking operations.

The Assam Rifles (52,500, 31 battalions) is a specialist force for counter-insurgency operations in the north-east. It maintains law and order in the tribal areas of Arunachal Pradesh, Nagaland, Tripura, Mizoram and Manipur, provides border security in the North-East, and conducts counterinsurgency operations.

In the event of an emergency, the paramilitary forces often get drawn into the situation. The Central Reserve Police Force and the Border Security Force have quite frequently been utilized in disaster situations. Recently, during the landslides in the Uttar Pradesh Hills, the Indo-Tibetan Border Police came forward in a big way to rescue the trapped victims (pilgrims) and provide relief to the affected population.

DEFENSE FORCES

India defense forces have made a significant contribution to the country in their principal roles of national defense, stability, and integration. The defense forces have engaged in operations against the Portuguese in Goa (1961), the Chinese (1962), and the Pakistanis (1947, 1965, 1971). Today they continue operations in border areas (vis Pakistan and China) and counterinsurgency operations in Kashmir and the North East states. Under the role of ensuring national stability, they have been used to provide disaster assistance during floods and earthquakes.[10] The Defense Forces are most useful in providing timely assistance such as dropping food, water and medicines to affected areas, erecting military bridge equipment and other services that save lives immediately.

The President of India is the Supreme Commander of the 1,145,000-strong armed forces (Army, Air Force, Navy, and Coast Guard), but responsibility for national defense rests with the Cabinet. Both operational and administrative control of the three services is exercise by the Ministry of Defense through the services. Within the State, the District Magistrate can requisition services of the Army in the role of "aid to civil power."[11] The Army, with 980,000 personnel, is the dominant service.

Army Field Formations include 5 Operational Commands (under Chief of the Army Staff in New Delhi) that command 11 corps: Northern (HQ Udhampur, with 2 Corps); Southern (HQ Poona, 2 Corps); Eastern (HQ Calcutta, 3 Corps); Western (HQ Chandimandir, 3 Corps); and Central (HQ Lucknow, 1 Corps). Each command is under a General Officer Commanding-in-Chief who holds the rank of Lieutenant General. The GOC-in-C commands a Field Army assigned to a geographical area, and has one or more corps assigned in defensive sector as well as static formations (administrative and support) under his command.

Static Formations of the Indian Army include Area and Sub Area Commands that maintain close liaison with civilian officials at the state and district levels. Area Command roles include construction projects (housing and water projects) and distribition of government funding for the various projects; running supply depots and services; and performing numerous administrative duties for the Army. Missions for employing Army forces during disasters can be tasked to the Area Commands.

The Air Force (110,000 personnel) is organized into 5 regional commands: Western Air Command (HQ New Delhi); South-Western Air Command (HQ Jodhpur); Central Air Command (HQ Allahabad); Eastern Air Command (HQ Shillong); and Southern Air Command (HQ Trivandrum). There are two functional commands, the Maintenance Command and the Training Command. The Chief of the Air Staff is at the apex with the Air Headquarters in New Delhi. The IAF operational inventory includes Mig-21, Mig-23, Mig-25, Mig-27, Mig-29, Jaguar and Mirage-2000 fighter aircrafts. The SU-30 fighter is the latest acquisition.

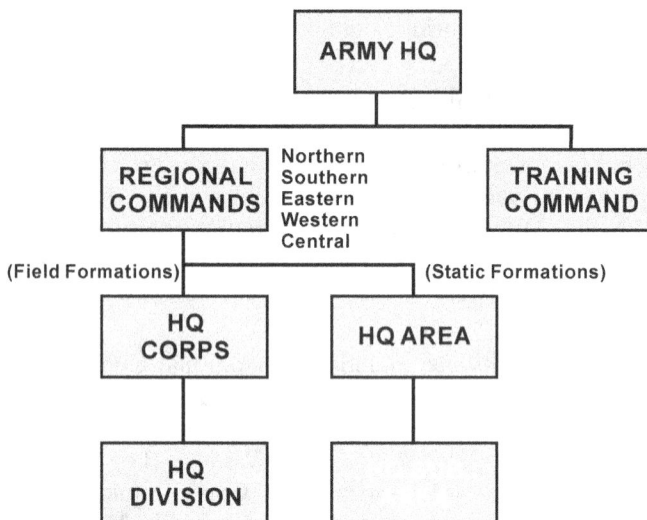

Figure IV-3, Army Organization. Source: *SP's Military Yearbook.*

The Navy (55,000 personnel) is responsible for the defense and security of India's maritime interests and assets, both in times of war and peace. The Chief of the Naval Staff at the Naval Headquarters, New Delhi has three commands: Western (HQ Mumbai); Eastern (HQ Vishakhapatnam); and Southern Command (HQ Kochi). Each command is headed by a Flag Officer Commanding-in-Chief in the rank of Vice-Admiral. The Western and Eastern Commands have operational fleets under them comprising warships, submarines, aircraft and other support ships. The Southern Command is responsible for all training activities.

The Coast Guard (4,080 personnel) was established by the parliament in 1978 to oversee India's coast line of 7,800 kilometers and adjacent Exclusive Economic Zone. It conducts anti-smuggling, search and rescue, and environmental support missions. The Ministry of Defense provides the administrative control of the Coast Guard, working through three Regional Headquarters located at Mumbai, Chennai, and Port Blair (Andaman and Nicobar Islands). The budget for the Coast Guard comes from the Department of Revenue, Ministry of Finance. The force structure includes 58 ships and boats and 32 fixed and rotary wing aircraft.[12]

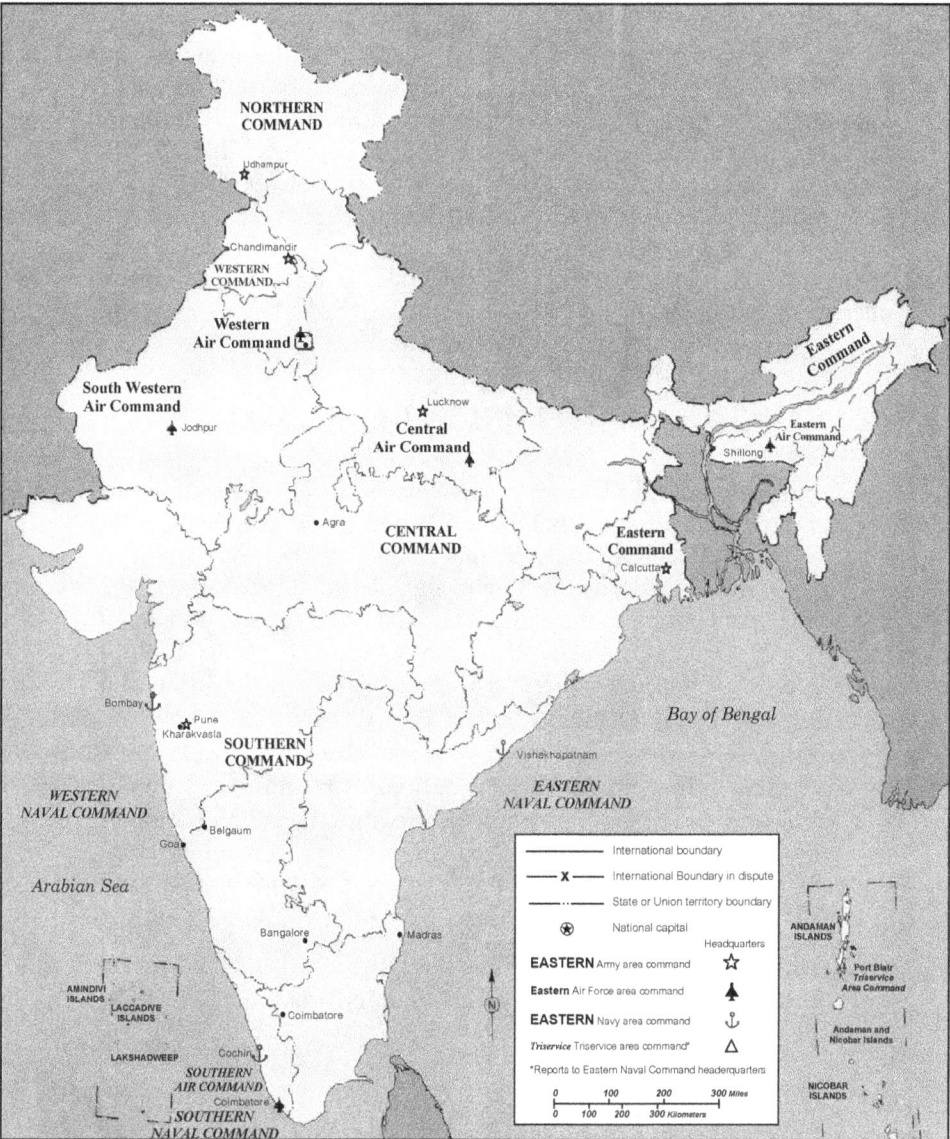

Figure IV-4, Army Areas. Source: *India A Country Study. Washington: Library of Congress, 1986.*

The Territorial Army (TA) is a voluntary part-time civilian force. It was raised in 1949 and has since then rendered valuable service, both in times of war and during internal disturbances. The Territorial Army has departmental and non-departmental units. The departmental units are raised from amongst employees of government departments and public sector undertakings. It has presently 56 units or battalions with a total strength of about 40,000. The units are Infantry Battalions, Railway Regiments, General Hospital (GH) Units, Indian Oil Corporation/Oil and Natural Gas Commission (IOC/ONGC) Units, Ecological (Eco) Battalions, Wasteland Development Units, and so on. Its Infantry Units have taken active part in military operations in 1962, 1965 and 1971 and have been employed for counter insurgency operations in the country. The TA's ecological units have done good work in converting bare land into forests.

ROLE OF THE ARMED FORCES IN DISASTER RELIEF

The armed forces of the country have played a vital role in times of disaster, providing prompt relief to the affected people even in the most inaccessible and remote areas of the country. The organizational strength of the armed forces, their high sense of discipline, the enormous manpower at their disposal and their excellent human resource management makes them an extremely useful tool in providing disaster relief. There are occasions when the scale and intensity of disaster goes plainly beyond the capabilities of the civilian administration.[13]

When placed into motion, Indian military operations to support disaster assistance are guided by agreed principles for military support to civil authorities that are also consistent with general military doctrine. Selected principles for military support to India's civil authorities are outlined here:[14]

- Armed Forces assistance will be requisitioned only when the situation cannot be handled by civil administration;

- When needed, the Armed Forces will provide immediate response;

- While responsive to the direction of civil authorities, the military chain of command will remain in place and in force;

- Aid will be requisitioned by civil authorities on a task (mission) basis;

- Liaison and coordination will be effected throughout the period of the assistance mission;

- Advance planning and training will be conducted;

- Military (and civilian) resources will be integrated as needed to effectively accomplish tasks;

- The Armed Forces will be released from the support mission as soon as the civil administration can take control of the situation.

The contribution of the armed forces in disaster management has generally been in the following spheres:

- *Search and Rescue:* The armed forces capability for aerial search and rescue is indispensable in the event of disaster in remote areas;

- *Communications:* The army have a very sophisticated communication network. These are utilized if there is a breakdown of the communication channels at the disposal of the civilian administration;

- *Debris Clearance:* The earth moving equipment with the defense forces is utilized to clear debris from the damaged areas and highways;

- *Evacuation:* The army help is sought particularly when people are trapped in inaccessible high altitude areas. Helicopters are pressed into service to evacuate the injured requiring medical treatment. The army fleet of vehicles come in handy in evacuating the people.

- *Medical Relief:* The Army Medical Corps has rendered signal service in providing medical relief to people affected by disaster;

- *Housing and Shelter:* The Army has the expertise to raise temporary hutments at short notice to accommodate people rendered homeless in the event of a disaster;

- *Roads and Bridges:* These invariably get damaged during a disaster. The engineering wing of the Army helps in repairing them or in constructing temporary bridges to facilitate the movement of goods and people;

- *Protection of Life and Property:* The Army assists the civil administration in maintaining law and order on specific request by the civil administration. This happens when the state police finds itself over-stretched and is not able to cope with the problems thrown up by a crisis;

- *Transportation:* The Armed Forces move supplies and personnel to and around the disaster site.

The support to disaster relief efforts provided by the armed forces was demonstrated during the earthquakes in Uttarkashi in UP (1991) and Latur in Maharashtra (1993). In Uttarkashi, the Army efforts were mostly in the remote hilly areas where there were no surface roads and the relief teams had to go up through tortuous and winding paths. The Air Force helicopters undertook sorties to rescue the injured persons and trapped tourists, and shift them to Dehradun. Medical teams were flown from New Delhi in Dornier aircrafts and taken deep into the interior villages by helicopters. The Indo-Tibetan Border Police (ITBP) deployed in the area also rendered commendable service. The Border Roads Organization helped in clearing the roads.[15]

In Maharashtra, the armed forces were quick to respond to the call of the State Government. On the very first day, the army helped in extricating a couple of hundred bodies and providing tent cover to about 10,000 people. The recovery equipment was utilized to clear the debris. Three field ambulance units, each capable of functioning as an independent hospital, were detailed to provide medical services. A total of about 10,000 people were treated by these units. The troops also established water points for about 45,000 persons and distributed cooked food in about 35 villages. The Navy's Western Command provided milk, water, food, tents, medicines and doctors. A satellite communication network was airlifted by helicopters to reinforce the communication system.

The Army personnel (with Air Force helicopters) rendered tremendous service during the recent landslides in the UP Hills also. They also helped the administration in flood relief operations in some states. In Uttar Pradesh, flood relief columns are located to cover the revenue divisions mentioned against them (see chart next page).[16]

The Army's Static Formations (Defense Forces above) play the primary role in providing support to civilian authorities during disasters. The Army Columns are placed at the disposal of civil administration on a formal request from the District Magistrate to the Station Commander or the Headquarters Sub Area.

As described in this chapter, there are considerable services available to support state and district officials to manage the consequences of earthquakes, storms, and other disasters. Yet, the

Columns at	Sub area (Source)	Civil Administration Divisions
Meerut	Meerut Sub Area	Meerut, Agra and Moradabad (less Rampur)
Meerut	Bareilly Sect.	Bareilly, Hill Sect., Moradabad (Rampur)
Mathura/Meerut	Lucknow Sub Area	Kanpur, Lucknow, Bareilly (Shahjahanpur)
Roorkee	Dehradun Sub Area	Dehradun and Garhwal
Jhansi/Meerut	Allahabad Sub Area	Allahabad, Faizabad, Gorakhpur, Varanasi, and Jhansi.

nature of disasters could overwhelm government's ability to rapaidly and fully respond to victims' needs. The next chapter will describe National, State, and local government organizations and processes for disaster management.

Endnotes

1. Ministry of Urban Development, *Vulnerability Atlas of India* (New Delhi: Government of India, 1977), Introduction.

2. "Disaster Relief Plan," U.S. Mission to India (New Delhi: U.S. AID, 9 March 1998), 15.

3. Ministry of Information and Broadcasting, *India 1998, A Reference Manual* (New Delhi: Government of India, 1998), 689. Also see "Public Health," *Statistical Abstract India 1997, 631-39.*

4. Ministry of Health and Family Welfare, *Annual Report 1997-1998* (New Delhi: Government of India, 1997), 13.

5.*India 1998* , 532. See also R. K. Jasbir Singh, *Indian Defence Yearbook 1998-99* (Dehar Dun: Natraj Publishers 1998), 393.

6. Singh, 395.

7. India 1998, 533.

8. Authors' notes. For comparison, Bureau of Police Research and Development, Ministry of Home Affiars, *Data on Police Organizations* in India (New Delhi: Government of India, 1998), 36, identified 1997 strength as 1,346,940.

9. Singh, 183, 372-82.

10. Jayant Baranwal, ed., *SP's Military Yearbook*(New Delhi: Guide Publications, 1997), 144.

11. D. P. Khanna, "Role of Administration, Army, Police, and Home Guards In Rescue and Relief Operations," *Earthquake Disaster Management* (Bhopal: Disaster Management Institute, 1998), 69.

12. Baranwal, 93-6.

13. Vinod K. Sharma, *Disaster Management* (New Delhi: National Centre for Disaster Management, 1997), 85.

14. Hema Ramaswamy, Memorandum, "The Indo-U.S. Seminar on Disaster Relief, March 12-15, 1997," U.S. Agency for International Development (New Delhi: U.S. AID, 14 April 1997), 6.

15. Indu Prakash, *Disaster Management* (New Delhi: Rashtra Prahari, 1994), 48-9.

16. Relief Commissioner, Uttar Pradesh State, to District Magistrates, 8 August 1998, authors' files.

_____

V. National, State and Local Levels of Government

Effective and accountable local authorities are the single most important institution for reducing the toll of natural and human-induced disasters...[1]

World Disasters Report 1998

Under India's federal system, the states have responsibility for disaster response. In the event of disasters which spread over several states or union territories or are otherwise of a grave nature, the Central Government supplements the efforts of the state governments by providing financial and material assistance.

By Government policy, calamities like earthquake, drought, flood and cyclone are regarded as major while hailstorm, avalanche, landslide, fire accident, etc. whose impact is localized and the intensity of damage is much less, are grouped as minor calamities. Measures required to meet these threats differ considerably in terms of disaster preparedness and amelioration of the economic and social life of the affected people.

- *Flood:* The Central Water Commission has established a warning system with a network of 157 flood forecasting stations on major inter-state rivers of the country. Flood forecast are issued to various State authorities to enable them take advance action to save life and property.

- *Drought:* The damage on account of drought is sought to be mitigated with drought proofing and other measures taken at the first sign of failure of rains.

- *Earthquake:* There is no reliable method of predicting the occurrence of an earthquake with respect to time and space but, seismologically, the earthquake prone areas could be identified and measures like construction of quake resistant structures and shelters, which help in mitigating loss of life and property, taken.

- *Cyclone:* A two stage cyclone warning system is available in the country to trigger advance precautionary measures in the face of cyclone threat. The first stage cyclone alert is issued 36-48 hours before the expected commencement of adverse weather by the

Cyclone Warning Center to the State Chief Secretary and the Collectors of the districts likely to be affected. Repeated broadcasts on the radio and television are also made to warn the people and advise them on the measures they should take. The second stage cyclone warning bulletin from the India Meteorological Department (IMD) is issued about 24 hours before the expected cyclone.

Minor calamities like hailstorm, avalanche, landslide and fire accident occur without any appreciable degree of forewarning. However, areas prone to such disasters could be identified and precautionary measures taken by way of promoting general awareness and formulating appropriate responses to particular calamities.

NATIONAL LEVEL

The extent of Federal response depends on the gravity of disaster, the scale of relief operations required, and the need of central assistance to augment the financial resources of the State. A government *Policy Response* to a natural calamity would be provided by the Prime Minister, Cabinet Committees and the Agriculture Minister. The objectives of policy response would be to address the sufferings of the people affected by the natural calamity, and to subserve long term and short term policy objectives of the government. A policy response could lead to visits to the calamity affected areas by Prime Minister and other dignitaries; setting up machinery for implementing, reviewing and monitoring the relief measures; and activating the administrative response process for assistance in relief measures.[2]

The *Administrative Response* by the Federal government relates to operational requirements and the provision of Central assistance in accordance with established policy. These operational requirements are seen as *primary relief functions* and *secondary relief functions*.

The Government's primary relief functions include these activities:

- Forecasting and operation of warning systems;
- Maintenance of uninterrupted communication;
- Wide publicity to warnings of impending calamity, disaster preparedness and relief measures through TV, AIR and Newspapers;
- Transport with particular reference to evacuation and movement of essential commodities and petroleum products;

- Ensuring availability of essential commodities at reasonable prices;

- Ensuring availability of medicines, vaccine and drugs;

- Preservation and restoration of physical communication links;

- Investments in infrastructure; and

- Mobilization of financial resources.

Secondary functions of the Central Government supplement the States' relief efforts, and they include these activities:

- Flood/inflow forecasts from the Central Water Commission;

- Relief, rehabilitation and restoration through military aid to civil authorities;

- Contingency plans for crops, cattle preservation, nutrition and health measures;

- Technical and technological inputs for provision of drinking water;

- Technical assistance in water budgeting and management; and

- Coordination of the activities of State agencies and voluntary agencies.

The Government of India's *Contingency Action Plan* for natural calamities defines the various organizational structures at the national, state and local levels which would handle disaster related matters in their respective jurisdictions, and lays down the policy guidelines to be followed by them. The Department of Agriculture and Cooperation (DAC) in the Ministry of Agriculture is identified as the nodal department for all matters concerning disaster relief at the Center. In the DAC, the Relief Commissioner coordinates the relief operations for all natural calamities. The organizational set up of the Scarcity Relief Division is shown in Figure V-1.[3]

The Central Relief Commissioner would receive information relating to forecast/warning of the natural calamity from the Director General, India Meteorological Department (IMD) or from the Central Water Commission. He also would send information up the chain of command to keep everyone informed: Secretary (Agriculture & Cooperation), Agriculture Minister, Cabinet Secretary and the

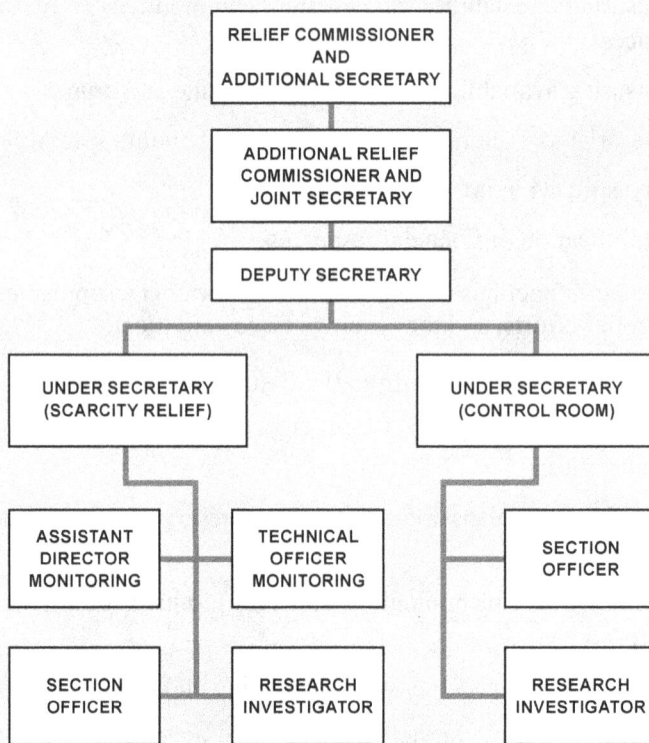

Figure V-1, Scarcity Relief Division. Source: Ministry of Agriculture.

Secretary to Prime Minister, and the Prime Minister (plus the Cabinet, Government Ministries and Departments, and the National Crisis Management Committee (NCMC)). The Relief Commissioner would also disseminate information to the State Governments for appropriate action.

The pattern of interaction amongst the different Ministries and Departments in the event of natural calamities is illustrated in Figure V-2.

The Relief Commissioner sets up an Emergency Operations Center (Control Room) on receipt of first information about the occurrence of a major natural calamity. The Control Room functions round the clock, collecting and transmitting information, keeping in touch with the

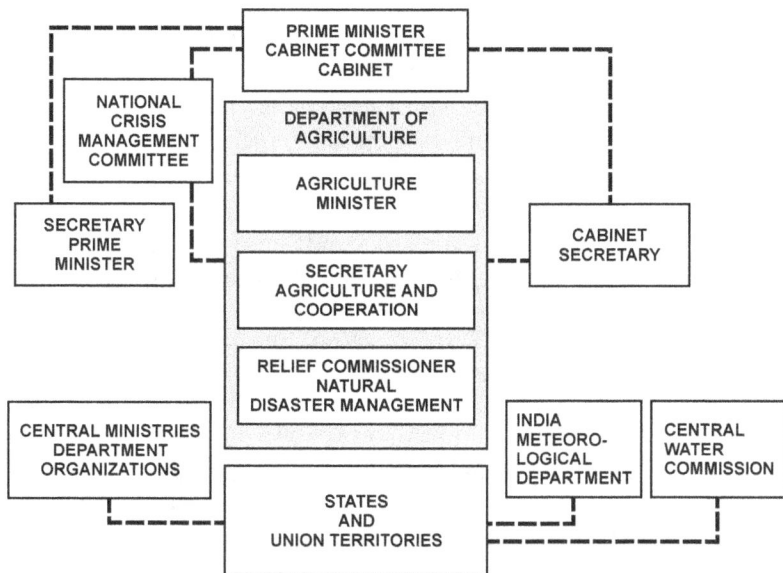

Figure V-2, Interaction Among Ministries and Departments.
Source: Department of Agriculture.

governments of states affected, and interacting with the Central Ministries and Departments to coordinate the relief measures. The Ministry of Agriculture's *Contingency Action Plan for Natural Calamities* outlines several committees at the national level active in disaster management policy and process:

- *Cabinet Committee:* The Cabinet may set up a committee for effective implementation of relief measures in the wake of a natural disaster. The Secretary in the Ministry of Agriculture acts as Secretary of this committee. In the absence of such a committee, all matters relating to relief are reported directly to the Cabinet Secretary.

- *National Crisis Management Committee (NCMC):* The NCMC is constituted under the chairmanship of the Cabinet Secretary as part of the Cabinet Secretariat. Other NCMC members are: Secretary to Prime Minister; Secretary, Ministry of Home Affairs; Secretary, Ministry of Defense; Director, Intelligence Bureau; Secretary (Research and Analysis Wing); and the Secretary, Agriculture and Cooperation.

•*Crisis Management Group (CMG):*   This group is headed by the Central Relief Commissioner and comprises senior officers drawn from various ministries and other concerned departments. The CMG reviews every year the Contingency Plans formulated by the Central Ministries and Departments; assesses the measures required for dealing with a natural disaster; and coordinates the activities of the Central Ministries and State governments pertaining to disaster preparedness and relief. The Additional Central Relief Commissioner is the convener of the CMG. The CMG meets at least twice a year in the months of December/January and May/June and as often as may be required by the Relief Commissioner.

Hazardous Substances Management

The Ministry of Environment and Forests is the lead agency for the management and control of hazardous substances—chemicals, waste and micro-organisms. Under India's Environment (Protection) Act of 1986, it has established rules concerning hazardous substances.[4]

The latest rules - Chemical Accidents Rules, 1996 - define chemical accident as "an accident involving a fortuitous, or sudden or unintended occurrence while handling any hazardous chemicals resulting in continuous, intermittent or repeated exposure to death, or injury to, any person or damage to any property but does not include an accident by reason only of war or radio-activity."[5]

The Central Government has constituted a Central Crisis Group for the management of chemical accidents and set up a Crisis Alert System in accordance with the provisions of the Rules. Some of the functions of the Central Crisis Group include rendering financial and infrastructure help, publishing a list of experts and officials concerned with chemical accidents, reviewing industrial emergency plans, and conducting post-accident analysis.

National Center for Disaster Management (NCDM)

The NCDM was established in 1995 by the Minister of Agriculture to provide a center for disaster coordination among government bureaus and Non-Government Organizations (NGOs) and a means of providing training on disaster management. "We are the interface between the Indian Government and the NGOs—and we are encouraging the states to prepare disaster management plans," advised Dr. Vinod K. Sharma, NCDM Professor of Natural Disaster

Management. The NCDM has a 13 member faculty of various disciplines such as behavioral science, social development, engineering and computer science.[6]

Currently, NCDM conducts 30 training programs for government employees and NGOs (e.g., CARE, OXFAM, Red Cross) in three training modules: training for actual disaster management practitioners; training for mid-level government leaders; and training for the senior heads of directorates. NCDM has an extensive publishing program that supports its mission. It makes use of the IIPA Library which contains over 180,000 volumes, and is one of the biggest libraries on Public Administration in Asia. "We have extensive holdings of Government of India Reports and Journals," explained Sunita Gulati, the Research Librarian.

A major project for the NCDM is the National Disaster Management Plan. "We are very good in the response part, but not good on planning; we are now working on a national policy for preparedness and mitigation," said Dr. Sharma. He expects to finish the Plan by 2001, with NCDM doing about half the effort of writing and staffing the plan. A major task is to coordinate and converge all the various Government of India policies and procedures into one document.

Council for Advancement of People's Action and Rural Technology (CAPART)

CAPART is a Government of India nodal agency under the Ministry of Rural Development to mobilize the voluntary organizations in disaster management. A January 1995 CAPART workshop on the subject of "Strengthening of Community Participation and Role of NGOs" emphasized collaborative relationships between voluntary organizations and the village *panchayats*, particularly in the context of delegation of powers and responsibilities to the village bodies.[7]

Regional CAPART- sponsored regional workshops on "building up national capability to cope with natural disasters" have since been conducted at Guntur (AP), Kanpur (UP), Mussoorie (UP), Nagpur (Maharashtra), and Konark (Orissa). Some of the broad recommendations which emerged out of these workshops included disaster management training programs, encouraging community action, establishing an Indian Society for Disaster Reduction, preparing case studies, and building a disaster management data base. In addition to Central Government organizations, there are many state, district and local crisis groups, institutes and local government organizations that play important roles. Arguably these are the most important of the

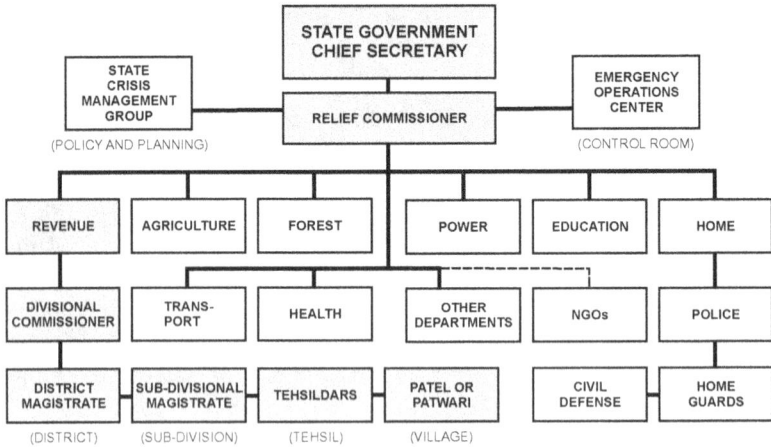

Figure V-3, State Disaster Management, Levels of Administration. Source: Authors.

organizations because of their proximity to the event and their constitutional mandate.

STATE LEVEL

The state governments in India are autonomous in organizing relief operations in the event of natural disaster and also for purposes of long term preparedness and rehabilitation measures. The Central Government's role is limited to supplementing the efforts of the state governments.

Every state has a Relief Commissioner who is in charge of disaster relief. In states where there is no designated Relief Commissioner, the Chief Secretary or an officer nominated by him is given overall charge of relief operations. Every state has a number of Secretaries who head various departments connected with administration and they all function under the overall supervision and control of the Chief Secretary, who ensures that their combined efforts are coordinated in disaster management. The states deal with natural disasters through their Revenue Departments or Relief Departments.

The states also have a State Crisis Management Group (SCMG) which function under the chairmanship of Chief Secretary / Relief Commissioner. The Group comprises senior officers from the departments of revenue / relief, home, civil supplies, power, irrigation, water supply, local self government (*panchayat*), agriculture, forests,

96

rural development, health, planning, public works and finance. The SCMG is expected to take into consideration the guidance received from the Government of India from time to time and formulate action plans accordingly for dealing with different kinds of natural disasters.

The Relief Commissioner of the state establishes an Emergency Operations Center (Control Room) as soon as disaster situation develops. The Center collects and disseminates the latest information on forecasting and warning of disaster, and functions as the focal point for coordinating disaster relief efforts with the other concerned departments.

Several states have been active in training disaster management personnel and preparing contingency plans. A good example is the Centre for Disaster Management at the Yashada Government Training Institue in Pune, Maharashtra. It is a research and training institution which has focused on assisting the districts with developing their distaster management plans. Among the states, Maharashtra has taken lead in preparing a comprehensive multi-hazard Disaster Management Plan (DMP). The plan has three components:

Risk Analysis and Vulnerability Assessment,
Response Planning, and
Mitigation Strategy.

The Risk Analysis and Vulnerability Assessment depicts the present picture for each disaster - exposure, loss of life, property damage, etc. It also shows geographic distribution of each hazard. The various monitoring facilities, regulatory regimes, and the countermeasures available for each disaster have been depicted in the analysis.

The Response Plan gives the organizational structure of all the state, central and non-governmental agencies to effectively deal with disaster in a coordinated manner to mitigate its impact. It identifies the functional areas such as relief, communications, information, transport, health services, etc. and proposes assignments to the various departments. The plan also lays down preparedness checklists, operating procedures and reporting formats.

The Mitigation Strategy focuses on the long-term planning for disaster reduction. It deals with issues of continued commitment to hazard identification and risk assessment, applied research and technology transfer, investment-incentives for mitigation, and leadership for mitigation. The strategy argues for better land use management, building codes, traffic standards, health standards, etc.

These objectives are to be secured through disaster legislation, mitigation regulation, and incentives for mitigation.

The Disaster Management Institute (DMI)

DMI at Bhopal, India was established in 1988 by the Madhya Pradesh state government as a follow up to the Bhopal gas tragedy, but it remains a semi-autonomous organization with the status of a separate legal entity. DMI it is an example of a hybrid professional organization involving both state government and private support.

DMI has a General Body headed by an Executive Director, with policy oversight provided by an Executive Council.[8] It supports itself through income from the sale of publications, consulting fees, membership fees, and sponsorship. For example, the Government of Norway provided a grant to "develop DMI as a Center of Excellence on issues pertaining to Chemical Accidents and Disasters."[9]

The DMI provides training courses and consultation assistance to industry and governments throughout India on matters of safety audits and reports, emergency planning, risk assessment and analysis, hazardous operations studies, and environmental audits. The current objectives of DMI are to organize and conduct technical training programs; create public awareness; contribute to the professional body of knowledge through documentation and dissemination of information.

The DMI training calendar includes a rich offering of courses on these subjects: Safety Audit and Environmental Audit; Air Monitoring, Analytical and Assessment Techniques; Management of Chemical Accidents; Earthquake Disaster Management; Characterization and Management of Hazardous Wastes; Environmental Management System; Environmental Assessment and Emergency Management Plan Formulation; Industrial Safety, Safety Audit, and Law; Management of Fire, Explosion and Toxic Releases in Industries; Hazard Analysis and Risk Management; Industrial Safety and Hazard Control; Safety Health and Environment Regulations, Management Approach; Management of Solid Wastes in Hazardous Industry; and Management of Chemical Accidents.

According to DMI Director, Dr. R. B. Sharma, emphasis is placed on the rehabilitation of disaster victims. Research and training looks at the physical, social, economic and psychological dimensions of rehabilitation. "There is little attention to what happens after a disaster," Sharma said. "The basic point of disaster recovery is the human dimension—we are often too concerned with the material." As an example, he described the Bhopal industrial disaster. The government has distributed some compensation, but still 14 years afterward there is no effort on the social-psychological aspects. The official figure was 4,500 dead on the first day, but the actual figure claimed by non-official organizations was four times as large, and there were large numbers of livestock that were lost. Now, the ground water around the Union Carbide chemical plant is contaminated.

DISTRICT LEVEL

Every state is divided into a number of districts. The head of the district administration is known as the District Magistrate or Deputy Commissioner. (In some states, he is better known as Collector). The District Magistrate is in charge of all the relief measures at the district level. The State government routes its instructions through him, and the District Magistrate ensures that the total efforts of the district are geared in a coordinated manner to providing disaster relief to the people. Sometimes, in emergency situations, the District Magistrate's powers are enhanced with a view to ensuring complete unison in the efforts of all the concerned departments.

A district is further divided into sub-divisions and tehsils. The head of the sub-division is called a Sub-Divisional Officer or Deputy Collector while the *tehsil* is headed by an officer called the *Tehsildar*. The lowest unit of administration is the village whose revenue matters are attended to by a functionary known as *Patel* or *Patwari*. All these tiers of administration - the *Patwari*, *Tehsildar*, Deputy Collector and the District Magistrate - function as a team to provide succor to the people in the event of a disaster.

The various measures undertaken at the district level are:[10]

- *Contingency Plans:* The District Magistrate develops a district level plan which is submitted to the state for approval. The plan assigns measures to be taken by the different District departments and their functionaries, and it identifies the areas of coordination.

- *District Relief Committee:* The relief measures are reviewed by the district level relief committee consisting of official and non-official members and including the local representatives of the people, members of the legislative assembly and the parliament.

• *District Control Room:* A Control Room is set up in the district as soon as a natural disaster occurs. The control room monitors the rescue and relief efforts on a continuing basis.

• *Coordination:* The District Magistrate also coordinates with central government authorities and defense forces that may be posted in the district. He synchronizes the voluntary efforts of NGOs with the efforts of the district administration. The communication channels are maintained through the police wireless network in the event of breakdown of the normal means of communication, the telephone and the telegraph.

The District level Contingency Plans and the State Action Plans are reviewed annually and updated in the light of lessons learnt in dealing with natural calamities. Copies of the revised/updated contingency plans of the State and the Districts are made available to the Ministry of Agriculture.

FINANCIAL ARRANGEMENTS

The Central Government does provide physical and financial resources to support relief efforts during and after disaster events. The scope of the Central Government's assistance is guided by these factors:

• The gravity of the disaster;

• The scale of the relief operation needed; and,

• The requirements for Central assistance to augment state resources.[11]

The arrangements for financing state governments in matters of relief and rehabilitation in areas affected by natural disasters are governed by the recommendations of the Central Finance Commission on the subject from time to time. The scheme for the period 1995-2000 is based on the recommendations of the Tenth Finance Commission. Under the scheme, a Calamity Relief Fund (CRF) has been constituted for each state with contributions from the central and state governments to undertake relief and rehabilitation measures. The annual allocations of the CRF to the various states are based on their trend of expenditure on natural calamities during the past ten years. The central share of CRF is released to the state governments in equal quarterly instalments.

A committee of experts and representatives draws up a list of items, expenditure on which alone shall be chargeable to the CRF. A state level committee headed by the Chief Secretary decides the norms of assistance under each of the approved schemes. The norms could be modified by the Ministry of Agriculture, if necessary.[12]

In addition, the National Fund for Calamity Relief (NFCR) has also been constituted to deal with calamities of extreme severity. The NFCR is available with the Government of India with an allocation of Rs. 7 billion for the period 1995-2000. The Fund is managed by the National Calamity Relief Committee, which is a sub-committee of the National Development Council headed by the Union Agriculture Minister. In normal circumstances, the state governments undertake relief and rehabilitation measures utilizing the annual CRF allocations. They can, however, seek additional assistance from the NFCR in the event of a calamity of severe nature.

Government response to natural disasters is gradually improving at all levels. Nevertheless, it is felt that there is a lot of scope for improvement and a more integrated policy is needed at the national level to take care of all the vital aspects of disaster management. Often Non-Government Organizations (NGO) have been on the scene to assist during disasters, supplementing or even supplanting government support. The NGOs are critically important for disaster assistance in India, and they are the subject of the following chapter.

Endnotes

1. International Federation of Red Cross and Red Crescent Societies, *World Disasters Report 1998* (Oxford: Oxford University Press, 1998), 19.

2. *Contingency Action Plan for Natural Calamities*, Natural Disaster Management Division, Department of Agriculture and Cooperation (New Delhi: Ministry of Agriculture, n.d.), 3-5.

3. *Contingency Action Plan*, 6.

4. For example: "Manufacture, Storage and Import of Hazardous Chemicals Rules, 1989"; "Hazardous Waste (Management and Handling) Rules, 1989"; "Manufacture, Use, Import, Export and Storage of Hazardous Micro-organisms / Genetically Engineered Organisms of Cells Rules, 1989"; and "Chemical Accidents (Emergency Planning, Preparedness, and Response) Rules, 1996."

5. "Forest Notification," *The Gazette of India*, Extraordinary, Part II, Sec.3(i), 1996, (New Delhi: Ministry of Environment, 1 August 1996), 13-22.

6. Dr. Vinod K. Sharma, Professor, Natural Disaster Management, National Center for Disaster Management (NCDM), Indian Institute of Public Administration (IIPA), interview by authors (New Delhi: 28 September 1998).

7. "Strengthening of Community Participation and Role of NGOs," Conference Report, Council for Advancement of People's Action and Rural Technology, Ministry of Rural Development (New Delhi: Government of India, January 1995), 20.

8. The General Body consists of a President (Chief Minister of Madhya Pradesh state (MP); Vice President (Minister of Environment, MP); Member Secretary, (Chairman of DMI and Secretary of Environment MP); the professional Members of DMI; Members of the Executive Council. The Executive Council is made-up of a Chairman (Secretary, Health and Environment, MP); Member Secretary (Executive Director of DMI); and

general Members (MP state Secretaries of Revenue, Finance, and Industries; Government of India Joint Secretary from the Ministry of Agriculture; industry representatives, and academic representatives).

9. Lokendra Thakkar, Manager for Awareness, Documentation, and Information, Disaster Management Institute, briefing to authors (Bhopal: 24 Sep 98).

10. Vinod K. Sharma, "Natural Disaster Management in India," *The Indian Journal of Public Administration* (July-September 1997): 770-1.

11. Hema Ramaswamy, Memorandum, "The Indo-U.S. Seminar on Disaster Relief, March 12-15, 1997," U.S. Agency for International Development (New Delhi: U.S. AID, 14 April 1997), 4.

12. Sharma, 768-9.

VI. NGOs, International Organizations, and Community Efforts

The role of NGOs is a potential key element in disaster management...the NGO sector has strong linkages with the community base, and can exhibit great flexibility in procedural matters vis-a-vis the government.[1]

Vinod K. Sharma
Disaster Management, 1997

There are NGOs and there are NGOs. I'm not impressed with the capabilities of the NGOs, not all of them are sincere. Many NGOs are motivated by desire for social recognition. They want to hog the limelight and gather funds–but 50 per cent of them are good.[2]

Central Government Disaster Management Official
New Delhi, September 1998.

Many of the Non-Government Organizations (NGOs) in India have come to play a very useful role in disaster management. They operate at the grassroots level and, by virtue of their close involvement with the community, can often have an edge over the government agencies. Mostly unencumbered by a large bureaucratic structure, they can offer rapid response and a willingness to adjust to the situation discovered on site.

NGO ROLES

There are many different types of volunteer organizations functioning in India, classified generally as International Organizations (IO), private volunteer or non-government organizations PVO-NGOs, grassroots (local) organizations, and so on. They offer immediately available communications within the disaster affected community, technical services, manpower, and financial support. Indian scholars have found it useful to categorize these organizations by their operating behavior and fields of expertise in this way:

•*NGOs with large resources, on-going operations:* These typically enjoy international support and can respond quickly with large amounts of supplies and services;

- *Development Technology related NGOs:* These may be involved in their own commercial research and development, but their equipment and expertise can be used in time of need in such areas as sanitation and building technology;

- *Interest Groups:* Groups such as the Rotary Club or the Lions' Club make resource contributions during disaster events;

- *Occupation Association:* These groups, such as a medical association, provide specialized services and generate specialized resources;

- *Residents' Associations:* These groups are highly motivated and an important means of mobilizing the local community. They generate community participation in disaster relief as well as planning and disaster mitigation efforts;

- *Religious Bodies:* These groups are immediately available to come to the aid of a community, offering capabilities for shelter and mass feeding;

- *Educational Institutions:* Private and government educational institutions play a critical role in reaching large parts of the population with information about preparing for and recovering from disasters. Their facilities can provide save havens for the homeless.[3]

Depending on their capabilities, organized action by them is useful in the following activities related to different stages of disaster management :[4]

- *Pre Disaster:* –Awareness and information campaigns
  –Training of local volunteers
  –Advocacy and Planning

- *During Disaster:* –Immediate rescue and first aid and psychological help
  –Food, water, medicine, other materials
  –Sanitation and hygiene
  –Damage assessment

- *Post Disaster:* –Reconstruction aid
  –Financial aid
  –Monitoring

India has a strong tradition of voluntary organizations responding to any calamity or disaster overwhelming the people. The voluntary organizations provide what no government agency is able to - relief and support with a human touch. There are such organizations spread all over the country.

During the recent 1998 cyclone in Gujarat, CARE-India provided food in the Khambhalia and Kalyanpur Blocks of Jamnagar districts for a period of two months and also gave 350 tents worth Rs. 700,000 in Jamnagar district. The OXFAM (India) Trust gave immediate relief in the form of food grains and plastic sheets and also provided clothing to over 1,000 families. The World Vision concentrated in Kutch district where the salt workers were hardest hit. They identified 250 families and provided them with roof tiles, wooden material etc. to reconstruct their houses. The Discipleship Center reached the Ropar and Bachau blocks of Kutch district within 72 hours of the disaster and covered around 870 families with emergency relief material. They also provided utensils and distributed plastic sheets, bed sheets, *sarees, dhotis* and children's clothing. CARITAS stepped into the areas within the first few hours of the calamity and concentrated on housing reconstruction.[5] The CRS, which works through the church organizations, provided US $ 10,000 for clean drinking water and shelter. Some 161 tonnes of food were also provided in Jamnagar, Porbandar, Dwarka and Kandla districts.[6]

NGOs WORKING IN INDIA

An annex to this report provides a listing of selected NGOs, but following is a sample of some the many NGOs working throughout India to provide a sense of the scope of their activities. The Ramakrishna Mission, with headquarters at Belur Math (Calcutta), has been extending, through its vast network spread all over the country, humanitarian relief to people in distress due to natural or man-made disasters. The Vivekanand Kendra, with headquarters at Kanyakumari (Tamilnadu), has also been active in this sphere, particularly in the north-eastern states. Larger organizations provide support throughout the subcontinent.

CARE (Cooperative for Assistance and Relief Everywhere) started working in India in 1950 when the Indo-CARE agreement was signed between the Government of India and CARE. The organization has since then supported many Government of India programs including the Mid-Day Meals, the Special Nutrition Program and Food For Work.

It has also been extending humanitarian assistance to save lives and reduce suffering caused by disasters. CARE-India provided relief assistance to the victims of earthquake in Maharashtra in 1993 and to the flood and cyclone victims in Andhra Pradesh in 1996. CARE-India is a member of the committee constituted by the Government of Andhra Pradesh for all rehabilitation and reconstruction projects in the State. CARE-India is also convener of the Government of India-NGO Committee on Emergency Preparedness.[7]

Under its current five-year Long Range Strategic Plan, CARE's goal is to increase women's control of their productive and reproductive lives. Major sector programs include Nutrition and Women's Reproductive Health; Women's Economic Empowerment; and Girls' Primary Education. CARE's staff of 370 people are working in the states of Andhra Pradesh, Bihar, Madhya Pradesh, Orissa, Rajasthan, Uttar Pradesh and West Bengal. Future efforts will include a CARE presence in Maharashtra and Delhi. At the state level, the CARE organization consists of a State Director, a number of sector program officers and a Finance and Administration Section.[8] CARE is prepared to work with Government of India organizations including the military, as well as with foreign and international organizations.

Humanitarian assistance is a part of CARE's sustainable development efforts. Its objective in providing emergency response support is to save lives and reduce suffering caused by disasters. CARE cannot provide disaster relief until requested to do so by the Indian Government. Because the CARE staff is already located in eight states, it is positioned to provide targeting and assessments for disaster management logistics and other support.[9]

CARE planning for disaster assistance involves two phases: an emergency phase involving rapid efforts to save lives and provide emergency food; and rehabilitation phase involving self-help projects. Attention is paid to predictive and preventive disaster planning issues. CARE plays an important role in distributing Public Law 480, Food for Progress Act, commodities and other emergency resources to state and local governments for emergency distribution.[10] During the rehabilitation phase, USAID and the Office of Foreign Disaster Assistance channel rehabilitation grants through CARE (as well as other agencies such as the Catholic Relief Services) to disaster victims.

CASA (Church Auxiliary for Social Action) was formed in the wake of the partition of India and constituted a Christian response to the human suffering engendered by that event. CASA's Peoples's Action for Transformation (PAT) program involves empowering people at the village level through Grass Root Level organizations such as Village Development Associations, Youth Groups and Economic Groups. To achieve sustained advancement of disadvantaged groups, village-level groups attack such issues as environmental degradation, deforestation, drought, migration, child labor, casteism, land encroachment, illiteracy, unemployment, indebtedness, pollution and so on.

Beyond the village, CASA organizes this effort at an intermediate level consisting of clusters of villages, and at a macro level involving a grouping of some 70 to 300 villages to form a Resource Center. The Resource Center is managed by a PAT Coordinator, three facilitators, an Accountant and a Caretaker. The Resource Center's goal is to equip people with the necessary information, skills and knowledge to sustain development at the village level. PAT Resource Centers are guided by four zonal offices. Overall, CASA reaches 6,033 villages via 7,048 Grass-roots Level Organizations.[11] CASA also has a vigorous schedule of direct development, educational, and disaster relief programs.

CASA responds to some 70-80 disaster emergencies yearly. Operational concepts include forecasting and warning of a calamity, education and training of people at risk, disaster plans, and the prestocking of nonperishable disaster relief materials in CASA warehouses at strategic locations. CASA defines operational phases of disaster response as Immediate Relief (alleviating immediate suffering via food, water, clothing, healthcare and shelter); Rehabilitation (restoring community equilibrium and rebuilding the means of sustenance); and Long-term Development (overcoming widespread poverty and helplessness).

As government disaster response communications may not be available to the NGOs, the critical importance of reliable communications is stressed by CASA. It is now in the process of developing a communications system of UHF, VHF, and satellite supported equipment that is intended to facilitate initial disaster assessment and rapid feedback to regional and national coordinators. This is important to CASA which relies on its own grass-roots network to identify needs and distribute materials.[12]

VHAI (The Voluntary Health Association of India) contributes to disaster mitigation and management in the field of public health. It has branches in each state and does its own disaster management planning at central and state levels. During the Maharastra earthquake of October 1993, it provided to the government a health status report which helped to guide public health recovery efforts. It publishes disaster management materials.

IRC (The Indian Red Cross) provides disaster relief as one of its services, rendering aid through a network of societies at the state level. The IRC maintains its own disaster assistance plan. It includes a survey of past disasters and training for staff and volunteers in disaster preparedness and relief operations.[13]

The IRC has established regional disaster relief operational headquarters at Guwahati in Assam and Ahmedabad in Gujarat with additional centers forthcoming at Vijayawada, Andhra Pradesh and in northern Punjab on the border with Kashmir. Other IRC disaster relief operational headqarters are located at New Delhi, Mumbai, Calcutta, and Chennai. Each headquarters will have a central warehouse of about 50 mt capacity, transportation fleet, communications center, and operations center.

Recent plans are to locate 30 medical and welfare centers, 30 mobile dispensaries, 6 state and 32 district-level warehouses (of 10 mt capacity) in the states of Assam, Bihar, Haryana, Orissa, Punjab, Tamil Nadu, Uttar Pradesh and West Bengal. The IRC has been a participating agency in the constructin of 227 cyclone shelters, each stocked with supplies for 350 people.

OXFAM (India) (Oxford Committee for Famine Relief) has served in India for over 25 years. Its goals include increasing food security, improving access to health and education, improving the lives of women, and improving India's disaster preparedness and mitigation. Seeking to alleviate poverty and hunger through a market-led, growth-oriented approach, OXFAM programs aim at India's most vulnerable groups. Some examples of these include marginalized rural communities, forest dependent communities, nomadic communities, urban poor, traditional artisans, fishing communities and people employed in unsafe and exploitative industrial and mining activities. OXFAM programs in India include supporting advocacy and public policy organizations; strengthening democratic institutions; helping vulnerable groups to access development resources; supporting producer groups with workshops on business management, exporting, and marketing.[14]

OXFAM United Kingdom and Ireland serves as the leading agency of OXFAM International in India. Recently, the OXFAM (India) Trust has been established and it now operates with funds raised in India. The National Office of the OXFAM (India) Trust is located in New Delhi, and it operates through six regional offices: Gujarat-Rajasthan in Ahmedabad, Gujarat; South India in Bangalore, Karnataka; Orissa in Bhubaneswar, Orissa; East India in Calcutta, West Bengal; North India in Lucknow, Uttar Pradesh; and Central India in Nagpur, Maharashtra.[15]

In working toward improving India's disaster preparedness, OXFAM representatives work with and through officials at the local level, district administrations, and in cooperation with NGOs and grass-roots organizations. This often entails working with the District Magistrate and the Superintendent of Police, India's typical first responders. OXFAM has an interest in tackling issues of the post-crisis period, such as long-term psychological trauma often evidenced by school dropouts, alcoholism and apathy. While many NGOs's focus on sustainable development, OXFAM staff have placed emphasis on health issues, sanitation, disabilities, and the long-term psycho-social aspects of disaster relief. They also recognize that the attention span of some agencies is short while the long-term effects of even a relatively small disaster may be severe. OXFAM planning includes concerns for industrial accidents, but it does not address nuclear disasters.[16]

Sambhavna Trust (Bhopal Peoples Health and Documentation Clinic) is an example of a locally run grassroots organization. It is tending to the long-term physical and psychological injuries of the Bhopal disaster victims within its limited resources. (A methyl isocyanate (MIC) gas leak at the Union Carbide factory on December 3, 1984 resulted in thousands of deaths of people on the first night and injuries to tens of thousands more–and there are continuing health problems for victims of the Bhopal disaster.) It is also collecting data about the Bhopal victims that may be useful to disaster management professionals, especially if these data can be properly recorded and analyzed in a computer-supported data base program.

Sambhavna Trust assists people visiting the clinic who present indications of various stages of impaired vision or blindness, problems with gastrointestinal disorders, problems with immune systems, post traumatic stress disorders, and women's reproductive health problems (menstrual cycles, stillbirths, and children with birth defects). In addition to dispensing commercial drugs, the Sambhavna Clinic is producing some 30 compounds (traditional or alternative medicines) that are being used to treat victims of the chemical accident. The clinic is attempting to study the effects of groundwater contamination and determine the extent of what is believed to be a serious problem.

UNITED NATIONS' ROLE

UNDP (United Nations Development Program) is responsible for coordinating disaster response operations that United Nations organizations would support or conduct in India. It is unlikely that the Government of India would ask the U.N. to coordinate a disaster assistance effort and the UNDP does not have a designated disaster officer, though a staff program officer is tasked to oversee coordination as needed.

UNICEF (United Nations Children's Fund) is an independently operating International Organization (IO) of the United Nations. With a child population of over 300 million, India is UNICEF's largest country program. UNICEF funds programs in mother and child health, water and sanitation, nutrition, primary education, and elimination of child labor.[17]

Since 1978, the Government of India has not made an international appeal for assistance in dealing with disasters, preferring to respond with its own resources and organizations. Nevertheless, UNICEF lends support to disaster assistance when it receives requests for assistance (typically from local level governments or organizations). The method for giving support during disasters is working through the Indian NGOs and local authorities. The UNICEF organization within India includes a central Country Office in New Delhi and eleven state offices.[18]

The United Nations General Assembly has also contributed to the field of disaster management. Through a resolution passed on December 11, 1987, it declared the nineties to be the *International Decade for Natural Disaster Reduction (IDNDR)*with the objective of reducing, "through concerted international action especially in developing countries, loss of life, property damage and social and economic disruption caused by natural disasters, such as earthquakes, windstorms [cyclones, hurricanes, tornadoes, typhoons], tsunamis, floods, landslides, volcanic eruptions, wildfires, grasshopper and locust infestations, drought and desertification, and other calamities of natural origin."[19]

The IDNDR established disaster reduction goals for the decade. These goals encouraged countries to improve their capacity to mitigate the effects of disasters, devise strategies for disaster management, encourage scientific and technological efforts and capabilities to assist in disaster reduction, and to develop various measures for disaster assessment, prediction, prevention and mitigation. The U.N. enjoined nations to participate in the Decade for Natural Disaster Reduction and establish a National Committee to promote and act as a focus for IDNDR activities.

At the World Conference on Natural Disaster Reduction held at Yokohama (Japan) from May 23-27, 1994 a strategy for the year 2000 and beyond was developed. It provided guidelines which emphasized prevention measures, self-reliance, education and training, and the networking of centers of excellence to enhance disaster prevention, reduction and mitigation activities.

India has been trying to follow the IDNDR guidelines. The concept is to make disaster reduction part of India's development plans so that recurring disasters will not erode progress in social and economic spheres. For example, the Indira Gandhi National Open University (IGNOU) in New Delhi has started a foundation course on Disaster Management in its School of Social Sciences to educate people on the subject. Also, the training institutions in several states have started special courses to equip their officers in the scientific techniques of Disaster Management. Directly as a follow up to the IDNDR Ykohama Conference, the government constituted the National Center for Disaster Management in 1995 under the Ministry of Agriculture.

DONOR COUNTRIES

The donor countries are important to India for supplementing the supplies and services offered by the NGOs. Contributions by these countries can be effectively employed in cooperation with or directly through the NGOs' organizational framework established throughout the country. The countries that typically may be called upon for disaster assistance include: Australia, Canada, Denmark, France, Germany, Great Britain, Italy, Japan (especially the Japanese Aid Agency), Netherlands, Norway, Sweeden, and Switzerland. United States disaster assistance (usually under the Public Law 480 Food Program) is managed by USAID, and it is provided through an NGO such as Catholic Relief Service or CARE. Disaster planners should contact the embassies of these countries for planning and assistance.

SELF-RELIANCE AND SOVEREIGNTY

The Indian Government is conscious of the need for self-reliance in responding to disasters, and, therefore, it does not normally request the direct involvement of foreign governments or donor agencies in the distribution of relief or monitoring of their disaster aid efforts.[20] As it does not like to call for international assistance, donor governments and

International Agencies should consider providing support through the offices of established Indian NGOs. This approach avoids bureaucratic impediments, increases the likelihood that materials go directly to the point of need, and does not challenge the policy of self-reliance.

When the Government informally requests assistance from donor nations and voluntary agencies, it may ask a volunteer agency (e.g.,OXFAM (India), Indian Red Cross) to coordinate donor aid in cooperation with the Ministries of External Affairs, Finance (Department of Economic Affairs) and other relevant agencies.

The United States' contribution to disaster relief in India is typically the provision of PL 480 foodstuffs and other commodities through the U.S. voluntary agencies CARE and Catholic Relief Services, which are designated cooperating sponsors under the Public Law 480 Title II (Food) Program.[21]

TIMELY, EFFECTIVE SUPPORT

Official responsibility for providing disaster assistance rests primarily with the state governments and, within the states, the District Magistrates. Nevertheless, the NGOs within India are instrumental in providing timely and effective support to people in need. The summary of selected NGOs provided above describes the wide variety of types of volunteer organizations available to assist and their capabilities. Professional expertise and material support come from religious groups, educational institutions, local grassroots organizations, technical enterprises, as well as the more formally established NGOs.

The Central Government has taken steps to include these NGOs in it disaster management training and operations. Under the Ministry of Agriculture, the National Center for Disaster Management is now working on a National Disaster Management Plan which will consider the important role of the NGOs.

Previous chapters have provided a review of India's geographical setting, infrastructure, and organization for disaster relief. The following chapter will provide examples of disaster management procedures and capabilities in India by way of description of disaster incidents.

Endnotes

1. Vinod K. Sharma, Joint Director, National Centre for Disaster Management, ed., *Disaster Management* (New Delhi: Indian Institute of Public Administration, 1997), 86.

2. Nonattribution interview by author of Government disaster management official, New Delhi, September 1998.

3. Anshu Sharma, Manu Gupta, and Amir Ali Khan, "Role of NGOs in Disaster Management," *Training of Trainers Programme on Disaster Management for NGOs*, Vinod K. Sharma (New Delhi: Indian Institute of Public Administration, 1997), C-28.

4. Vinod K. Sharma, "Natural Disaster Management in India," *The Indian Journal of Public Administration* (July-September 1997): 772.

5. CARITAS is the Latin word for charity. CARITAS is a world-wide service organization of the Catholic Church.

6. "Response to the Gujarat Cyclone Situation," Minutes of NGOs Meeting held in New Delhi on July 20, 1998, author's files.

7. CARE, "50 Years CARE," CARE, India pamphlet (n.d.).

8. Harry S. Sethi, Director, Special Projects, CARE-India, interview by authors, New Delhi (22 Sep 98).

9. Peter McAllister, Assistant Country Director, CARE-India, interview by authors, New Delhi (22 Sep 1998).

10. Public Law 480 (P.L. 480) also known as the Food for Peace Program. The P.L. 480 food aid program is comprised of three titles. Each title has different objectives and provides agricultural assistance to countries at different levels of economic development. Title I of the P.L. 480 program is administered by USDA, and Titles II and III are administered by the Agency for International Development (AID). P.L. 480 programs are entered into to combat hunger and malnutrition; promote broad-based equitable and sustainable development, including agricultural

development; expand international trade; develop and expand export markets for United States agricultural commodities; and to foster and encourage the development of private enterprise and democratic participation in developing countries. Title II provides for the donation of U.S. agricultural commodities by the U.S. government to meet humanitarian food needs in foreign countries. Commodities may be provided to meet emergency needs under government-to-government agreements, through public and private agencies, including intergovernmental organizations such as the World Food Program, and other multilateral organizations. Non-emergency assistance may be provided through private voluntary organizations, cooperatives, and intergovernmental organizations. See U.S. Food Aid Programs Description, Internet <http://151.121.3.140/excredits/pl480/pl480ofst.html>.

11. Church's Auxiliary for Social Action (CASA), "CASA," pamphlet (New Delhi, 1997).

12. Santosh Clare, Material Aid Officer, Church's Auxiliary for Social Action, interview by authors (New Delhi, 22 Sep 1998).

13. "Disaster Relief Plan," U.S. Mission to India (New Delhi: U.S. AID, 9 March 1998), 21. Information provided in this section by U.S. AID, New Delhi.

14. "OXFAM at Work in India," Internet, <org/oxfam/atwork/where/asia/india.htm>, accessed 3 Oct 1998.

15. "OXFAM UK and Ireland Field Office Address Book," Internet, org/oxfam/atwork/intaddr.htm, accessed 3 Oct 1998.

16. Unnikrishnan P. V., M.D., OXFAM (India) Staff, interview by author, New Delhi, 23 September 1998.

17. Peter Delahaye, Deputy Director (operations) and Mr. S.S. Alam, Procurement Officer, UNICEF, interview by authors, New Delhi: 23 September 1998. "UNICEF in India," Internet <www.giftsnaccessories.com/unicef/index.htm>, accessed 1 Oct 1998.

18. UNICEF-India offices are located at: Bangalore, Karnataka; Bhopal, Madhya Pradesh; Bhubaneswar, Orissa; Calcutta, West Bengal; Chennai, Tamilnadu; Gandhinagar, Gujarat; Hyderabad, Andhra Pradesh; Jaipur, Rajasthan; Lucknow, Uttar Pradesh; Mumbai, Maharashtra; Patna, Bihar.

19. "International Decade for Natural Disaster Reduction," Resolution 44/236, 45th Session, U.N. General Assembly, 22 December 22 December 1989; available from <http://www.aber.ac.uk/~jpg/hazards/idndrres.htm>; Internet; accessed 20 January 1999.

20. *U.S. Mission to India Disaster Relief Plan* (New Delhi: USAID, 9 Mar 1998), 17.

21. Heather W. Goldman, Ph.D., Director, Office of Social Development and Mission Disaster Relief Officer, interview with authors (New Delhi: 23 September 1998).

VII. Examples of Disaster Response

It [Bhopal] was a lesson that nobody wanted to learn...[1]

R. B. Sharma
Director, Disaster Management Institute
Bhopal, 1998

Previous chapters have provided background on India's environmental setting, its infrastructure, service organizations, and established procedures for managing disasters. In this chapter, several cases of disasters occurring in recent years provide insight into Indian planning and response. These incidents underline the importance of effective disaster management to a country where, almost every year, a number of natural and man-made forces threaten lives and property. In 1997-98 alone, the damage due to natural calamities was as follows:[2]

Damage to crop area (in million hectares)	15.37
Damage to houses/huts	1,330,849
Human lives lost	2,373
Animals lost	28,111

Andhra Pradesh had the largest crop area (4.73 million hectares) affected due to flood, drought, cyclone and hailstorm followed by Karnataka (3.61million hectares) where the damage was caused by flood, drought and pest attack. The largest number of houses/huts damaged were in Madhya Pradesh (548,693) due to flood, heavy rains, earthquake and hailstorm followed by Bihar (201,390) where the damage was caused by flood and hailstorm. The maximum loss of human lives was in Andhra Pradesh (305) followed by Gujarat (285) and Maharashtra (273). The largest number of animals lost were in Jammu & Kashmir (6,682) followed by Gujarat (5,788).

The years 1998 and 1999 were particularly bad for the country from the point of view of disasters.Floods affected several states, particularly Assam, West Bengal, Bihar and Uttar Pradesh. Cyclones of severe intensity devastated Gujarat and Orissa. Landslides took a heavy toll of human lives in the hill regions of Uttar Pradesh. Incidents of flooding, drought, earthquake, industrial accident, cyclone, and landslides that have occurred in recent years illustrate the magnitude of the challenge to disaster managers.

FLOOD

There were unprecedented rains in Punjab, Haryana, Himachal Pradesh and Jammu & Kashmir in September 1988.[3] The worst hit districts were Amritsar, Jalandhar, Gurdaspur, Kapurthala, Ludhiana, Hoshiarpur and Ropar in Punjab. In Kapurthala, the water from Beas river submerged about 150 villages under 8 to 12 feet of water. In Jalandhar, fifty per cent of the standing crops were destroyed. In Ropar, thousands of people were trapped in flood waters and had to spend several nights on the rooftops of their houses. Gurdaspur town had two to four feet of water.

Figure VII-1, Northern Flood Areas in 1988.
Source: Map derived from *Oxford Atlas*, p.17.

In Himachal Pradesh, Kinnaur, Una, Chamba, Kulu and Shimla were badly affected. Roads at several places were breached and more than a dozen bridges in different parts of the State collapsed. About two thousand persons were marooned in the Pong dam area. Una was completely cut off. People living in Chamba along the Ravi river had to be shifted to safer places. The Grand Trunk Road between Beas, Rayya and Khalichain was submerged under three to four feet of water. Border Security Forces personnel were marooned at their outposts.

It subsequently came to light that over 405 thousand cubic feet per second (cusecs) of water was flowing in river Sutlej on September 24 against its capacity of 305 thousand cusecs. The additional 100 thousand cusec was released from the Bhakra Dam. The Bhakra Beas Management Board (BBMB) unfortunately did not warn the district authorities or the people before the release of water - and this aggravated the magnitude of the disaster. The miscalculation took place because deficient rainfall had been forecast for the month of September. Accordingly, the Bhakra reservoir was filled up by September 13. However, the Bhakra area received 85 mm of rain within 45 minutes only on September 26. The reservoir attained the highest ever level of 1687.47 ft., which was above the maximum storage level of 1685 ft. designed for the dam. There was panic about the safety of the dam. The BBMB therefore released the extra water without bothering about the capacity of the reservoirs below. People in areas downstream were caught unawares. As a result, there was loss of life and property on a massive scale.[4]

There have been other instances also of flash floods being caused due to release of water from the dams. The compelling reason for such releases have been the deteriorating conditions of the catchment areas. In the Himalayas, there is soil erosion on a large scale due to increasing deforestation and urbanization leading to the reservoirs getting silted and, as a consequence, their storage capacity being reduced and even the life span cut short.

The Government of India formed a Crisis Management Group under the chairmanship of the Relief Commissioner to coordinate the relief operations. The administration worked round the clock to restore road traffic, construct temporary bridges and organize rescue and relief operations. The voluntary agencies also came forward. The Army, Air Force and Border Security Force personnel worked with tremendous dedication to mitigate the effects of disaster. The Army's Western Command Headquarters directed its field formations in Punjab to render all necessary help to the civil authorities. The Army helicopters evacuated the men, women and children marooned in Berian village in the Pathankot sub division. Motor boats were sent to rescue 25 Gujjar families marooned in Majri village. The Indian Air Force provided seven helicopters for assistance in the states of Punjab, Haryana and Himachal Pradesh. Another five choppers were kept in a state of readiness at Chandigarh. The helicopters dropped 66,000 pounds of flour and pulses (peas, beans, lentils), rice, gram, bread, salt, milk powder and tea to the stranded populace.[5]

A voluntary body known as Flood Relief Society was formed with Justice Ajit Singh Bains, a retired judge of the Punjab and Haryana High Court, as Chairman to provide relief to the flood affected people of Punjab. The Society made Sikh and Hundu temples the focal points for collecting relief material. Charitable institutions were also associated. Medicines were distributed to prevent any outbreak of epidemics.

The 1998 floods affected large areas of northern and eastern states. Assam experienced the kind of flood which the state had not witnessed since 1950.[6] As many as 20 out of a total of 23 districts were under floods. Dhemaji in Upper Assam was the worst affected. Nearly 5,000 villages were submerged, and a total of 3.6 million people were affected by the fury of the Brahmaputra river. About 221 thousand hectares of cropped area was damaged.[7] Majuli, the largest river island in the world, was completely submerged and over 100 thousand people living on the island had to be evacuated. The Kaziranga National Park was flooded, forcing herds of one-horned rhinoceros, wild buffaloes and numerous species of deer to flee to high grounds in the neighbouring Karbi Anglong district and the nearby tea gardens. Preliminary reports indicated that nearly 31 rhinos and 5 elephants were drowned. The other animals which died included 20 buffaloes, 429 hog deer, 8 swamp deer, 10 sambars, 17 wild boars and one bear.[8] The State received about Rs. 420 million from the National Calamity Relief Fund.

In West Bengal, the flood situation threatened to overtake a similar catastrophe which happened in South Bengal in 1978. All the major rivers flowed above the danger mark in Malda, North Dinajpur, South Dinajpur, Jalpaiguri and Cooch Behar districts.[9] In Malda, 1.5 million people which is more than half its total population, were rendered homeless. Large areas of Murshidabad were inundated by the Bhagirathi river. The Army and the Border Security Force personnel assisted the State administration in the rescue and relief operations. The Navy also sent boats and a team of 50 people including doctors to Malda.

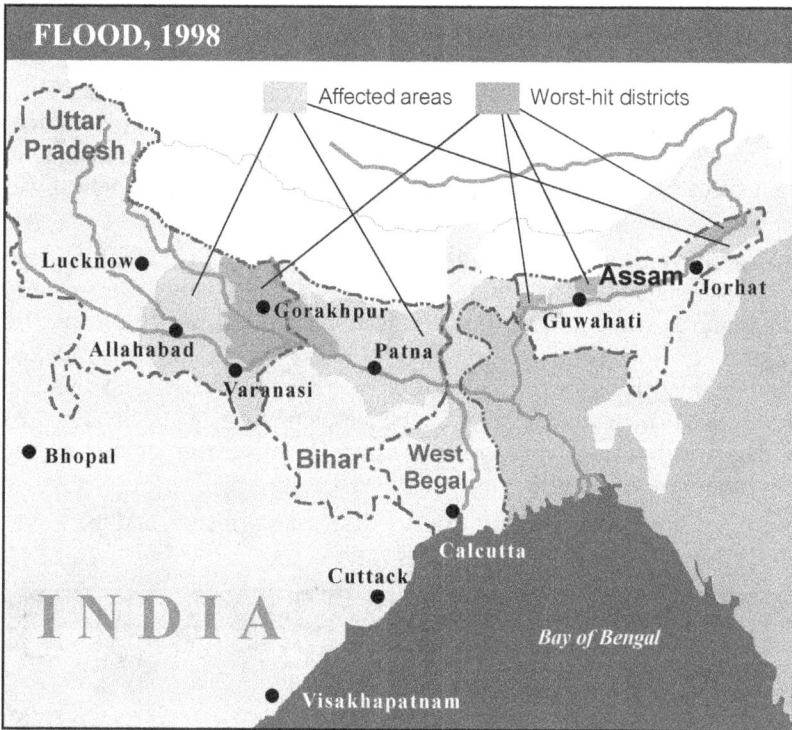

Figure VII-2, Eastern Flood Areas, 1998.
Source: *India Today*, Sept. 21, 1998, p.29.

In Bihar, vast areas in Saharsa, Katihar, Darbhanga, Purnea, Madhubani, Samastipur, and Monghyr were submerged under flood waters. A total of nearly 12 million people in over 7,200 villages in 28 districts in north and central Bihar were affected. The floods washed away standing crops worth more than Rs. 2.95 billion spread over an area of 1451 thousand hectares. Army personnel assisted in relief works in Katihar and Darbhanga districts.

In Uttar Pradesh alone, floods took a toll of over 1,000 lives in 51 of the 83 districts affected. Gorakhpur district in eastern UP was worst affected with its 1,187 out of 1,579 villages being marooned. The Air Force undertook Exercise FROG (Flood Relief Operations: Gorakhpur). The Army was also pressed into service and boats and boatmen were flown from Allahabad and Varanasi to give Gorakhpur an improvised public transport system.[10] The Center sanctioned Rs. 3 billion to the State for the relief programs. The Prime Minister also announced that talks were being held with the Government of Nepal to evolve a joint project for flood control. This was necessary as several rivers originate from the Himalayan Kingdom. It has been suggested the government should enter into various collaborations with Nepal with a view to constructing reservoirs, dams and canals at places near the source of rivers. One such project - the Pancheshwar dam - is, in fact, already being constructed on the Kosi river between Pancheshwar in Nepal and Pithoragarh in Uttar Pradesh.

There were floods in Madhya Pradesh, Orissa, Arunachal Pradesh and Meghalaya also, though its severity in these states was comparatively less. In Madhya Pradesh, flash floods washed away 500 houses in the Chhattisgarh region. In Orissa, the districts of Jharsuguda, Balasore and Sambalpur were affected. Arunachal Pradesh had heavy landslides due to incessant rains. In Meghalaya, 123 villages in the low-lying areas of Garo Hills were inundated by the Brahmaputra river, affecting 90,000 people.[11]

According to estimates, the casualties, areas affected, and the losses in the states worst affected were as follows:[12]

States	Death Toll	Districts Hit	Loss (Rs. in Billion)
Assam	150	21	10
West Bengal	165	8	10
Bihar	350	28	9.3
UP	1,000	55	28

The frequency and the severity of floods in India are generally attributed to the massive cutting of trees in the catchment areas of the Himalayas, high degree of sedimentation in the rivers, absence of any dredging operations, inadequate provision of spillways for the excess rainwater and the non-completion of flood protection measures. "People are not surprised by nature's fury, they are far more incensed by the recurring story of callousness and corruption which hold out little hope of a long-term strategy to alleviate the misery."[13]

Interestingly, floods caused havoc in China and Bangladesh also. The Yangtze river in China caused extensive devastation in 29 provinces, autonomous regions and municipalities and submerged 21 million hectares of land. Over 2,000 lives are reported to have been lost and the damage is estimated to be around US $ 21 billion. In Bangladesh, an estimated 30 million people were rendered homeless and about a million acres of crops damaged. More than 600 people died and there was a mass outbreak of diarrhoea.[14]

It is significant that even while overwhelmed by its own natural disasters, India has come forward to assist other countries in times of their distress. The country donated 20,000 tonnes of rice worth nearly Rs. 220 million to help Bangladesh tide over the flood crisis. Essential medicines worth about Rs. 4 million were also sent. Earlier, relief was extended to Afghanistan during the earthquake there.

DROUGHT

In his descriptive book on *Disaster Management: Societal Vulnerability to Natural Calamities and Manmade Disasters, Preparedness and Response,* Dr. Indu Prakash describes the drought of 1987 (caused by the failure of south-west monsoon) as one of the worst of the century.[15] Eighteen out of 35 meteorological sub-divisions received deficient rainfall. The overall deficiency during the monsoon period was (-)19%.

As soon as it became apparent that the drought was likely to have an adverse impact on agriculture, the Prime Minister set up a Cabinet Committee on Drought (CCD) with the objective of ensuring timely and prompt relief measures. The Department of Agriculture and Cooperation coordinated the efforts. The CCD formulated an Action Plan, the salient features of which were:

- Preparation of water budgets to optimize the use of water available in the reservoirs and utilization of ground water resources;
- Supply of adequate power in the agricultural sector so as to minimize crop losses;
- Provision of adequate drinking water;
- Strengthening the public distribution system (PDS);
- Public health measures; and
- Ensuring availability of fodder for the cattle.

Nearly 93 million out of 285 million affected people all over the country belonged to vulnerable sections of the society comprising small farmers, agricultural laborers, etc. Priority was therefore given to the generation of employment opportunities. The Government of India laid down the following order of priority in the selection of works: (1) tube wells, (2) ponds, (3) field channels, (4) soil conservation, and (5) laying of roads. The government also identified 94 major and medium and 19 minor irrigation projects in the drought affected states with a view to insulating agriculture in those areas in future from the vagaries of monsoon.

The state and local governments paid special attention to improving the availability of food-grains through the Public Distribution System. During the period ending July 1988, over one million tonne each of rice and wheat were allocated to the states. Steps were also taken to import 200 thousand tonne of pulses, 30 thousand tonne of butter oil and 30 thousand tonne of skimmed milk powder under various programs. Nearly 7,740 additional fair price shops were opened in the drought affected areas. Mobile vans were commissioned to supply essential commodities in the remote areas.

The management of drought of 1987 showed that the strategy followed in different parts of the country had certain common features: emphasis on employment generation, water conservation, contingency crop planning, public distribution of essential commodities and special nutrition programs, particularly for the weaker sections of society. There were however regional variations depending on the resources of the state, the behavior of monsoon over its geographical area, and the administrative capability of the state. The governments at the central and state levels were, on the whole, quite successful in tackling the drought. This has been attributed by Dr. Indu Prakash to the following four factors:

- A highly developed system rooted at the local community level but extending in an integrated way to the most senior levels of the Central Government;

- The ability of the meteorologists to forecast weather patterns, enabling the authorities to take timely action to mitigate the adverse effects;

- The concerted response of the central, state and local governments to the emergency. It is significant that within a few days of the prediction of drought, the Prime Minister chaired a special cabinet meeting where the strategy to deal with the impending crisis was chalked out;

- The dedication of the people who worked tirelessly in relief efforts at all levels.

EARTHQUAKE

The earthquake in Uttarkashi (Uttar Pradesh) on October 20, 1991 measured 6.1 on the Richter scale, though the seismological center in Colorado (US) gave its strength as 7.1. It rocked all the hill districts of the State, and the tremors were felt as far as Delhi, Chandigarh, Shimla and Jammu.[16]

The Bhatwari and Dunda sub-divisions of Uttarrkashi district were completely devastated. Electricity was disrupted. Telecommunication lines broke down. Most of the roads connecting the villages were breached and the wooden bridges collapsed. A statement made in the parliament revealed that 1,819 villages covering a population of 422 thousand were affected, and 768 lives were lost. About 20 thousand houses were damaged, and cattle loss was estimated at 3,000.

The State Government machinery swung into action to deal with the disaster. The Divisional Commissioner was stationed at Uttarkashi to supervise the relief and rescue operations. A control room was set up at Dehradun. The Agriculture Production Commissioner was entrusted with the rehabilitation of the earthquake victims. He was particularly directed to generate employment opportunities on a large scale under the Jawahar Rozgar Yojana.

The Crisis Management Committee of the Central Government with representatives drawn from various ministries including Agriculture, Civil Supplies, Surface Transport, Finance, Defense, Communication and Health took stock of the situation and prescribed the management strategy. A sum of Rs. 700 million was given as Calamity Relief Assistance to the State Government to meet the immediate requirement of the victims. The National Housing Bank was directed to extend loan assistance of Rs. 300 million for the repairs of damaged houses in the area.

There were nevertheless allegations that the government response was tardy and that the relief supplies reached very late. Besides, what was distributed was of poor quality and in paltry quantity. The official apparatus did not show sensitivity to the sufferings of the people.

Another major earthquake in recent times was in the Latur and Osmanabad districts of Maharashtra on September 30, 1993. It measured 6.4 on the Ritcher scale. The epicenter was close to village Killari in Latur district. Killari had experienced tremors earlier in 1962, 1967, 1983 and 1984. In 1992, it experienced no less than 125 tremors between August and October. It is learnt that the Government of Maharashtra had taken a decision to relocate the villages, but before the plan could materialize the tragedy occurred. There was extensive damage to life and property in the districts of Latur and Osmanabad with 7,928 people losing their lives and 16,000 suffering injuries. 15,847 livestock also perished. A total of 52 villages were razed to the ground and, as a result, nearly 27,000 houses were totally damaged.

The response from government as well as non-governmental organizations was prompt. A Control Room was set up in the Secretariat and the immediate tasks were identified. These included rushing Police and State Reserve companies to the area, arranging supply of drinking water, milk, medicines, mobilization of equipment for the removal of debris, restoration of communications, and requisitioning the assistance of Army's Southern Command and Navy's Western Command. Voluntary agencies contributed substantially to the relief efforts. Foreign assistance to the tune of over 3 million dollars was routed through the Red Cross.

The Government of Maharashtra formulated a comprehensive Maharashtra Emergency Earthquake Rehabilitation Program (MEERP) with the objective of rehabilitation of the earthquake affected people in the 52 villages of Latur and Osmanabad districts. The program envisaged socio-economic rehabilitation of the community and developing them as independent self-sustaining units. The total project, estimated to cost Rs. 11.82 billion, is financed by the Government of Maharashtra, Government of India and various international agencies like the World Bank, Department for International Development (DFID), United Nations Development Program (UNDP) and the Asian Development Bank in the form of loans, grants, donations and technical assistance.[17]

Jabalpur in Madhya Pradesh had an earthquake of magnitude 6 on the Richter scale on May 22, 1997. The greatest impact was felt at the junction of the Narmada and Mahanadi Rivers, where 39 people lost their lives and 2,421 sustained injuries in house collapse. Apart from Jabalpur City and district, villages of three other districts, namely Mandla, Seoni and Chindwada were also affected. In all, over 15,416 families were rendered homeless. The relief and rehabilitation efforts left much to be desired.

On March 29 and 30, 1999, an earthquake measuring 6.8 on the Richter Scale devastated Chamoli and Rudraprayag districts in the Garhwal division of the Uttar Pradesh Hills. One hundred people were killed and thousands were rendered homeless. This was the second major natural disaster in the Garhwal Hills within six months.

The personnel of the Indo-Tibetan Border Police (ITBP) and Border Roads Organization cleared the arterial roads and provided succor to the people. The Army evacuated the injured by helicopter, air-dropped relief supplies, and provided medical aid through its own teams.

The Union Government announced a relief package for the affected people. Rs. 100,000 each would be paid to the families of those killed who were earning members, while Rs. 50,000 would be paid to the next of kin of the non-earning victims. Commenting on the relief efforts, *India Today*, a leading magazine of the country, in its issue of April 12, 1999, commented as follows: "As for disaster management don't look beyond the tired, inadequate knee-jerk reactions."

CYCLONE

Gujarat was lashed by a severe cyclonic storm on June 9, 1998. According to the latest estimates available, a total of 1,250 people were killed while over one thousand were reported missing. Most of the casualties were those of the salt workers. There was devastation on a large scale in the districts of Kutch, Jamnagar, Rajkot, Porbandar, Junagadh, Amreli, Bhavnagar, Banaskantha, Surat, Bharuch, Valsad and Navsari. Nearly 66 hectares of agricultural land was eroded and thousands of trees were uprooted. About one hundred thousand tonne of salt was washed away in Kandla and the nearby areas. The gateway along the Gulf of Kutch became a graveyard of vessels with 40 ships having run aground and five of them actually sinking. The cyclonic storm hit western Rajasthan's border districts of Barmer, Jalore and Bhilwara also; there were 15 casualties, mostly as a result of house collapse and electrocution.[18]

The Gandhidham Chamber of Commerce estimated that the overall loss to the industry was to the tune of Rs. 12 billion, the major losers (in Rs. billion) were:[19]

Gujarat Electricity Board	5.31
Reliance Industries	2.00
Kandla Port Trust	1.32
Gujarat Maritime Board	1.16
Salt Industry	1.25
Rice exporters	1.00
Transporters	1.00
Timber industry	.53
Essar Refineries	.20
Irrigation projects	.06

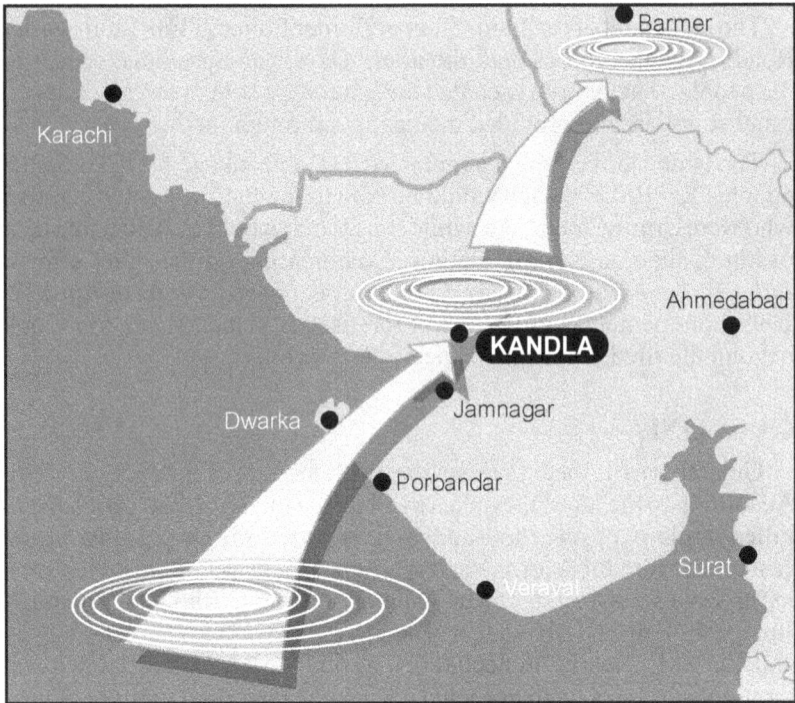

Figure VII-3, Gujarat Cyclone, 1998.
Source: *India Today*, June 22, 1998, p 32.

There were allegations that Gujarat's disaster management machinery did not rise to the occasion. *India Today* commented that the government reacted with a "caterpillar-like pace." In the State Assembly, the Congress members, during discussions on the tragedy, harped on the point that a majority of lives lost on June 9, 1998 along the Saurashtra-Kutch coastline could have been saved had the State Government implemented a sound disaster management plan. The Union Home Minister conceded that the cyclone forecast of the Meteorological Department had gone awry as there was no mention in its forecast that Kutch district, which was worst affected, would be hit. There was also lack of communication between the Kandla Port Trust Authorities and the district administration.[20]

It also came to light that the Kandla Port Trust had been repeatedly warned about the consequences of tampering with coastal ecosystems. Minutes of the Expert Appraisal Committee (EAC) of the Ministry of

Environment on July 27, 1995 had recorded concern that too many projects were coming up in the Kandla Port area. Political considerations had led to project after project being cleared. What was worse, the Government of Gujarat had even altered the Coastal Management Plan to facilitate projects in the Coastal Regulation Zone (CRZ). Thus, Reliance Petrochemicals were allowed to run an oil pipeline through the Marine National Park. The Indian Oil was allowed to set up a floating oil terminal at Vadinar, which began leaking oil into the marine ecosystem, damaging the plant protection barriers such as mangroves. Tragically, the salt industry, whose workers suffered the most from cyclone, added to this destructive process by stripping extensive mangrove habitats to make salt pans. Old timers confirm that since time immemorial tidal waves in Kutch had been tempered by a combination of natural barriers formed by coral outcrops, sand banks, mangrove plants and dunes. "In recent years, however, a virtual frenzy of chemical facilities, petroleum complexes, cement factories, ports and jetties have stripped these natural ramparts. That is why - with virtually nothing to impede the 200 km/h cyclonic winds and four-meter tidal waves - such a large number of innocents died."[21]

The Government of India decided to give assistance to the maritime states in the Ninth Plan for the protection of critical reaches of coastal areas. Under this scheme, the coastal areas would be protected by constructing sea walls. The Coastal Protection and Development Advisory Committee (CPDAC) has prepared a comprehensive National Coastal Protection Project (NCCP) estimated to cost Rs. 16 billion.

The State of Orissa was lashed by a super cyclone with windspeed estimated at a staggering 150 to 300 kms. per hour on October 29, 1999. It was accompanied by heavy rains and tidal waves that rose 4 to 6 metres. The cyclone devastated 12 coastal districts of the State. Paradeep port, which bore the brunt of the fury, was rendered unserviceable. The death toll was over 10,000. Property worth Rs. 10 billion was damaged. About 100 thousand hectares of forests, including mangrove forests, were destroyed and more than 9 million trees uprooted.

The Union Government released a grant of Rs. 5 billion as cyclone relief from the National Fund for Calamity Relief. The Prime Minister constituted a task force headed by the Defense Minister to direct and coordinate all Central rescue, relief and rehabilitation measures. Several countries came forward to help. The total financial commitment from the UN is around $ 500,000. The US President announced $ 2 million worth of food and $ 100,000 worth of tents and plastic sheeting. Denmark sent a consignment of 1,000 blankets for distribution through the UNICEF. The Pope, who was in India those days, also announced a donation of $ 300,000.

The Armed Forces of the country launched a massive relief effort. The Army cleared several National Highways and roads in the affected areas and helped in the restoration of surface communications. The Indian Air Force airlifted relief material to the marooned people. Indian Navy ships carried rations, medicines and other equipments. In a remarkable display of national solidarity, some state governments came forward to "adopt" the cyclone hit districts for undertaking relief and rehabilitation of the affected people. Thus, Maharashtra government adopted the worst-affected Jagatsinghpur district, Andhra Pradesh adopted Ganjam district, Madhya Pradesh adopted Jajpur, and Delhi took Puri district.

The cyclone and its aftermath nevertheless demonstrated that disaster management has a long way to go in India. The civil administration, instead of rising to the occasion, virtually collapsed and but for the timely help of neighbouring states and the Central intervention, the agony and suffering of the Orissa people would have been indefinitely prolonged.

LANDSLIDE

Landslides have recently caused havoc in the hill regions of Uttar Pradesh. On August 18, 1998, a massive landslide wiped out the entire Malpa village in the Pithoragarh district of Uttar Pradesh, killing about 210 people. These included 60 who were on a pilgrimage to Kailash-Mansarovar (Tibet) which is believed by the Hindus to be the abode of Lord Shiva. Eight personnel of the Indo-Tibetan Border Police (ITBP) also lost their lives. Earlier, 69 people were killed in devastating landslides in the Ukhimath block of Rudraprayag district on August 12. There were landslides in the Ukhimath area again on August 19, killing 26 people. There were casualties due to landslides in other areas of the region also: six were killed in Dehra Dun, five in Pauri, three in Srinagar, two in Khirsu, and two in Taroli. In all, according to *India Today,* a total of nearly 400 people are estimated to have been killed and 12 villages were wiped out in a series of landslides spread over a period of ten days in the hill regions of Uttar Pradesh.[22]

The State Government announced an ex gratia of Rs. one hundred thousand each to the next of kin of those killed in the tragedy and Rs.

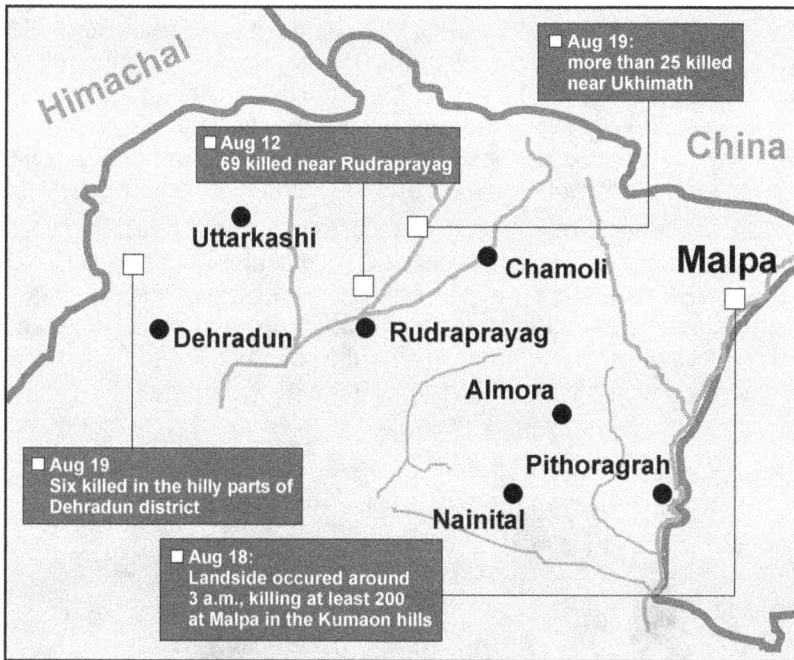

Figure VII-4, Landslide Disaster, 1998.
Source: *India Today* August 31, 1998 p.33.

50,000.00 each to the injured, and Rs. 25,000.00 for the reconstruction of damaged houses. A team of 200 personnel of the Army, Indo-Tibetan Border Police (ITBP), Pradeshik Armed Constabulary (PAC) and Border Security Force (BSF) was rushed to Malpa to carry out the relief operations. The Defense helicopters carried out sorties even in inclement weather to rescue the trapped persons and retrieve the dead bodies which could be located.

The community response was spontaneous. A correspondent who toured the region commented that the Ukhimath community "set a stellar example in altruism."[23] Every family fed at least one person affected by the landslides. "We take it that every family has one more member to look after," as a student of the Garhwal University said. The *Yuvak Mangal Dal* and the *Mahila Mangal Dal*, voluntary associations of youth and women in the region, did yeoman's service in rushing to the unsafe areas with succor. The Himalayan Environment Studies and Conservation Organization (HESCO), an NGO, sent medicines and relief materials.

Landslides are generally caused by a combination of weak, unstable geological formations and heavy rain. But, as has been rightly said, in many cases "man-made factors - such as the destruction of forests and other vegetative cover, indiscriminate mining and construction, disruption of drainage pattern, heavy use of explosives -provide the real trigger for the destructive torrent of rocks, rubble, soil and debris."[24]

It is unfortunate that in spite of recurring landslides in the region, adequate attention has not been paid to planning and preventative measures. A recent report by the Tata Energy Research Institute states that the cumulative effects of deforestation, erosion, water-logging, salinity and nutrient depletion all over the country have so far led to a staggering economic loss of approximately Rs.232 billion.

> *The tragedy is that despite a wealth of data and numerous experts in the field, there is very little planning going on. The tragedy is that it is the construction lobbyists and the Mafias dealing in Himalayan timber and stone, working in league with the politician and the administrator, who finally get to set the agenda for development in this region. Meanwhile, the forgotten people of the region continue to die as their land slips from under them and their houses collapse over them.[25]*

In view of the highly destructive potential of landslides in the Himalayan region, it is important that the government takes steps to prevent their recurrence. The high hazard zones should be carefully identified and proactive measures taken. These should include afforestation, increasing other green cover, having proper drainage, providing nets to trap debris, and imposing severe restrictions on destabilizing activities like use of explosives and indiscriminate construction works.

TECHNOLOGICAL DISASTER: BHOPAL

The Bhopal gas tragedy, which took place on December 3, 1984, was the worst technological disaster of the country. It was the result of faulty design, poor maintenance and unsatisfactory plant operation.

Union Carbide, a U.S.-based multinational company, had a plant manufacturing Sevin and other pesticides at Bhopal. Sevin is manufactured by taking methyl isocyanate (MIC), itself manufactured

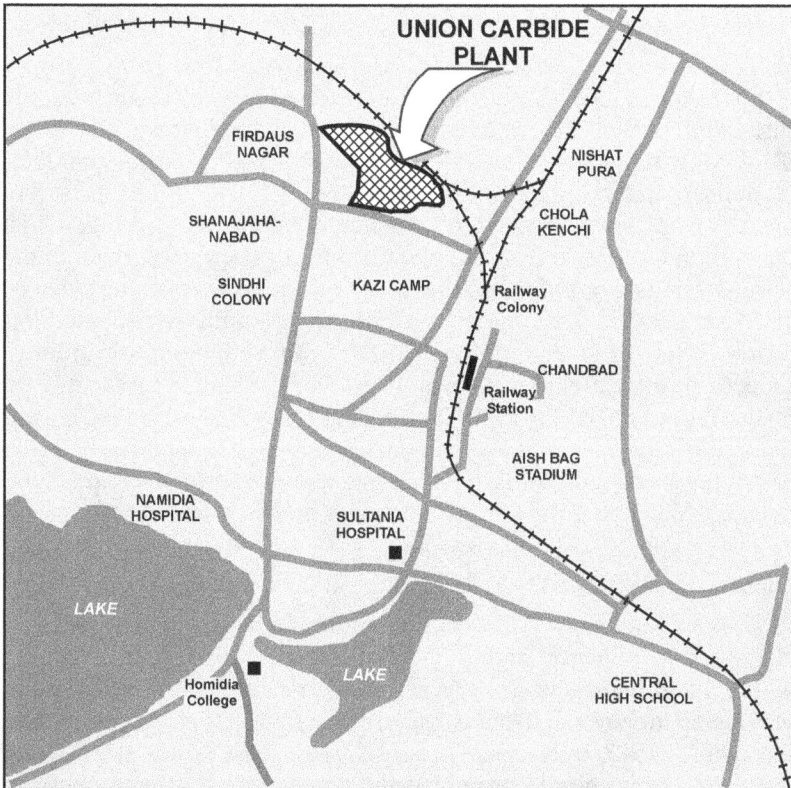

Figure VII-5, Bhopal and Union Carbide Plant.
Source: based on Larry Everest, *Behind the Poison Cloud,
Union Carbide's Bhopal Massacre.* Chicago: Banner Press, 1986.

by reacting methylamine with phosgene, and reacting it with alpha-naphthol.

On the night of December 2, the shift supervisor asked an operator to wash the piping around one of the three MIC storage tanks. As the valves on the tank leaked at times, a slip blind was inserted to seal off the tank and prevent any ingress of water. Initially it was felt that water had entered through this line though, as subsequent inquiries showed, it had actually entered via the nitrogen pressure line. The new shift operator noticed that there was a rise in pressure in Tank 610, but he thought that this was perhaps due to nitrogen pressure. Meanwhile, temperature and pressure continued to build up in Tank 610. Water was sprayed but it proved ineffective. The increasing pressure ultimately burst the rupture disc and blew the safety valve. As a result, MIC gas rushed straight through a 33 meter high atmospheric vent line into Bhopal's cool air.

Siren was sounded, but this made matters worse because people rushed out of their homes to put out what they thought was fire in the plant - only to inhale the gas. The town was turned into a gas chamber. "It appears that no practice drills were ever held. The various safety devices were never checked to see whether they were working, whilst the community living near the plant had never been warned about the serious dangers, or trained so that they knew what to do in the event of an emergency."[26] The tragedy, according to preliminary estimates, left nearly 3,000 dead and some 250,000 with permanent disabilities. Indeed, the exact figure is difficult to establish, and many estimates are in the range of 16,000 to 18,000 deaths related to the incident, not including livestock.[27] The maximum casualties were reported from the low-lying areas of the Old City including a shanty town of about 12,000 people which had grown up near the gate of the factory.

The Bhopal disaster was caused by a complex set of interdependent human, organizational, and technological factors: [28]

Human Factors. The working environment of the Bhopal plant "tolerated negligence and a lack of safety consciousness among workers and managers. Employee morale was low because the plant was losing money and being considered for divestment... According to the plant's 1982 operational safety survey, basic rules were being ignored... Low morale prompted the company's best employees to leave. In the four years prior to the accident, 80 per cent of the workers trained in MIC technology in the United States had left the plant. The others remained because they were local residents reluctant to leave the city."[29] In this environment, some of the unsafe practices and decisions involving breach of policy which contributed to the tragedy were as follows:

- The number of operators manning the MIC unit was cut to half between 1980 and 1984;

- Operators had inadequate safety training;

- Managers and plant workers had little information on the hazard potential of the plant, and there were no emergency plans;

- When storage tank E-610 failed to pressurize on October 21, 1984, managers did not investigate causes of the failure;

- Operators failed to put in a slip blind to prevent water from entering the storage tank during the flushing operation.

Organizational Factors. The Bhopal plant was an unprofitable unit in an unimportant division of the corporation. The plant represented one of the fifty international subsidiaries of Union Carbide representing less than two per cent of the parent company's world wide sales and less than three per cent of its profits. As an unimportant plant, it received fewer resources and less managerial attention which, in turn, made it less safe.

Besides, the parent company had made basic mistakes while setting up the plant. Union Carbide's executives had serious reservations about its economic viability and at one stage even considered abandoning the project. However they had advanced too far ahead to retrace their steps. In February 1984, James Law, Chairman of the Union Carbide Eastern division, proposed to sell off the plant with the exception of the MIC unit. The proposal was endorsed by the Carbide's top management but meanwhile the disaster took place.

The frequent changes and the inexperience of the top management was another contributory factor. The plant had been run by eight different managers over a period of fifteen years preceding the disaster. What was worse,

> *The need for... [contingency] ...plans was not identified, either by the local management or by the experts from headquarters who conducted the periodic operational safety surveys. This, in turn, contributed to the general lack of understanding, both in the plant and in the community, about the lethal nature of MIC*[30]

As many of the managers came from non-chemical backgrounds, and had little or no experience of dealing with hazardous technologies, there was a lack of urgency in preparing for dangerous accidents at the plant.

Technological Factors. The important technological factors which contributed to the disaster were in the design, equipment, supplies and operating procedures. These have been summarized by Paul Shrivastava in his *Bhopal : Anatomy of a Crisis* in the following words:[31]

Design. A number of design errors directly contributed to the disaster:

- Computerized early warning system and data logger were not incorporated into the design;

- Process design allowed for long-term storage of very large quantities of MIC in tanks;

- Water sprays were designed to reach only 12-15 m although gases from the flare tower were released at 33 m;.

- Jumper line design modification connected relief-valve vent header and process-vent header, allowing water ingress into storage tank;

- Maximum allowable scrubber pressure was 15 psi while the rupture disk allowing gas to come into the scrubber was rated 40 psi;.

- A single-stage, manual safety system was used in place of an electronically controlled four-stage backup safety system used in other similar plants;

- The design did not provide a backup system to divert escaping MIC to an effluent area for quick neutralization as in Bayer's MIC Plant;

- Manual system used for scrubber start up is generally less reliable than automatic systems.

Equipment. Equipment failures showed the need for maintenance and training:

- New plant was built in 1981 but poorly maintained;

- Instruments and gauges were unreliable;

- Valves and pipes were rusted and leaking;

- Refrigeration unit (30 tn capacity) was too small and erratic to be effective in case of runaway reactions;

- Safety and operating manuals were in English, not easily readable by operators.

Supplies. Supply factors also demonstrated poor training:

- Highly toxic MIC and phosgene gases used as basic raw materials without knowledge of their effects;

- MIC in tank E610 was contaminated with a higher chloroform level than allowable.

Operating Procedures. These proved to be fatal:

- Failure to pressurize tank E610 with nitrogen was ignored repeatedly;

- Refrigeration unit was shut down several months before accident;

- Flare tower and scrubber were simultaneously non-operational while large inventories of MIC were in storage;

- Spare tank was not empty for operators to transfer MIC to it;

- Tank E610 was filled to 75 to 80% of capacity. Recommended capacity was 50%;

- Water flushing of pipes was reordered without investigating what was preventing water from coming out at the other end.

It was the combination of these human, organizational and technological factors which combined to precipitate the tragedy.

Response. The doctors in Bhopal were called upon to treat the thousands of dying victims in what has been described as "an amazing environment of ignorance and even disinformation."[32] They did not know what had happened at the plant or how the leak had taken place. They did not know what gas had affected the people. And they did not know what was the treatment if it was MIC The Union Carbide officials compounded the problem by insisting that the MIC was only an irritant and not lethal. The local doctors, in any case, had no experience of treating patients affected with methyl isocyanate. And so they treated the patients on the basis of symptoms exhibited by them: eye drops for the eyes, steroids against inflammation, antibiotics to prevent secondary infections, antacids for the stomach, and oxygen respiration in acute cases. The treatment touched only the fringes of the ailment.

The Union Carbide managers knew well before the tragedy how dangerous the substance methyl isocyanate was. *A Preliminary Report for the Citizens Commission on Bhopal* brought out by Ward Morehouse and M. Arun Subramaniam has revealed that as far back as 1963, confidential research was undertaken for Union Carbide at the Mellon Institute at the Carnegie Mellon University in Pittsburgh on the toxicity of methyl isocyanate. The research, described in a confidential special report to Carbide, concluded that "methyl isocyanate appears to be the most toxic member of the isocyanate family" and that it "is highly toxic by both the peroral and skin penetration routes and presents a definite hazard to life by inhalation.[33] A subsequent research undertaken in 1970, also at the Mellon Institute, reinforced the earlier findings with additional data that MIC is highly toxic–even at very low vapor concentrations. The Carbide officials avoided safety responsibilities before the incident and, after the disaster, they suppressed the facts to minimize their culpability.

The government's response was unfortunately inadequate. The District Magistrate ordered closure of the factory and got five officers of the Company arrested. Doctors were rushed from other places. Teams of chemical industry experts and environmental experts were flown from Delhi. Officers of the Central Bureau of Investigation (CBI) also reached Bhopal. But, as commented in *No Place To Run : Local Realities and Global Issues of the Bhopal Disaster*,

> .....apart from these pedestrian and routine bureaucratic responses, the state or central government did precious little. Except for the Army, there was no help coming to the thousands who fled from their homes that morning. The government's centralization and lack of initiatives, so visible on ordinary days, became such a heavyweight around it in those critical days that it collapsed under stress. Individuals within the administration did work themselves to the wall but there was no overall planning. In those first few hours, reports suggest that there was complete confusion.[34]

The people's minds were full of misgivings - about the air they breathed, the water they drank and the meat and vegetables they ate. The government officials, instead of taking the people into confidence, issued contradictory statements from time to time. For example: "The water is safe, but boil it before drinking; vegetables and fruits are safe but wash them well before eating." The All India Radio did not project the correct picture when it broadcast that the situation was fast returning to normal and that everything was safe. It was rightly said that some official statements sounded like pronouncements of the Carbide officials. The *Operation Faith* launched by the government in the wake of the disaster was criticized as by some as "Operation Fake." The measures taken for medical treatment of the people, and their relief and rehabilitation were–and are today–inadequate.

Larry Everest, in his *Behind The Poison Cloud*, has given the following critical summary of Bhopal tragedy :

Was the disaster in Bhopal an accident, as it generally has been referred to in the US media? Yes, in the sense that it was not inevitable that such a disaster should take place in Bhopal; and nothing predetermined the disaster's timing, or the precise sequence of events involved. But in a more fundamental sense, the disaster was not accidental: the logic of profit maximization and imperial domination shaped all the various components of the catastrophe - from the plant's design and location, to its day-to-day operational procedures and whole history, to the way the corporation reacted on the night of horror itself, to its actions in the wake of the gassing. In this sense, the disaster in Bhopal was not so much a tragedy as a crime; not so much a 'unique combination of unusual events' as a horrifying and concentrated illustration of the essential operation of imperialism; not so much an accident as a massacre.[35]

An Action Plan of the State Government of Madhya Pradesh for the medical, economic, social and environmental rehabilitation of the Bhopal gas victims was approved by the Government of India for a period of five years from April 1, 1990 to March 31, 1995. Subsequently, it was extended to September 30, 1998. The outlay for the Action Plan was initially Rs. 1.63 billion but it has since been enhanced to Rs. 2.58 billion.

Global Repercussions. Chemical companies around the world were alarmed at the dimensions of Bhopal tragedy. Lest they were overtaken by any such event in their own establishment, they reviewed the existing safety devices and the emergency response procedures. Some of them even reduced the storage toxic chemicals and initiated a program of educating the area residents about the hazards. The risks of operating in developing countries were also reconsidered.

In the United States, the Chemical Manufactures Association undertook two industry-wide safety initiatives - the Community Awareness and Emergency Response program (CAER) and the National Chemical Response and Information Center (NCRIC). The CAER program aimed at giving the people basic information on hazardous chemicals through data sheets, lists of hazardous substances and hazard communication programs. The NCRIC extended the existing Chemical Transportation Emergency Center. Four news services were added : a round the clock information line for emergency service; CHEMNET, a mutual aid network of chemical industry and private emergency response teams; the Chemical Referral Center to serve as a focal point for information on chemical hazards; and development of training material for local emergency service personnel outside the industry. Besides, the Environmental Protection Agency (EPA) initiated the Chemical Emergency Preparedness Program (CEPP) to provide information on the most hazardous chemicals produced in the country and guidelines for communities to prepare emergency plans in collaboration with the local authorities and industry.

The Bhopal experience also prompted legislative initiatives around the world. Laws were enacted in Britain, France, Netherlands, Belgium, West Germany and in India. The Ministry of Environment and Forests in the Government of India came up with the following two important documents to regulate the growth of hazardous industries in the country :

- *The National Environment Tribunal Bill:* The Bill provides for strict liability for damages arising out of any accident occurring while handling any hazardous substance, and for the establishment of a National Environment Tribunal for effective and expeditious disposal of cases arising out of such accident with a view to giving relief and compensation for damages to persons, property and the environment, and for matters connected therewith or incidental thereto;

- *Ministry of Environment and Forests Notification:* This subjects industries to an Environmental Impact Assessment of each project along with a necessary Environment Management Plan for the prevention, elimination and mitigation of the adverse impacts from the inception stage of the project itself.

Judicial Settlement. The Supreme Court of India, in 1991, approved a $ 470 million (Rs. 715 crores) settlement between the Government of India and the Union Carbide Corporation as compensation for the disaster victims of Bhopal. This was much less than $ 3 billion sought by the Government. Of the 15,310 death claims adjudicated till April 1998, only 5,097 were awarded compensation of the following amounts as death cases:[36]

Compensation amount more than Rs. 300,000:	19
Compensation amount more than Rs. 200,000:	76
Compensation amount more than Rs. 100,000:	<u>5002</u>
	5097

The remaining 6,375 were awarded only injury compensation. Satinath Sarangi, Chief of the Bhopal Peoples' Health and Documentation Clinic, Sambhavna Trust, Bhopal, describes the sums awarded as cruel mockery as many of the victims will be sick for the rest of their lives. According to Sarangi, there are at least 125,000 people who are in an acute state of ill health as a result of a whole range of diseases like breathlessness, eye problems, neurological disorders, menstrual and other reproductive abnormalities, anxiety, depression and obstructive pulmonary disease.[37]

Lessons. The lessons to be learnt from the Bhopal tragedy, as brought out by Martin Abraham of the International Organization of Consumers Union are useful for consideration during disaster management planning. Abraham's observations and suggestions are as follows:[38]

- Hazardous production facilities pose added risks in Third World countries, where skilled labor and public awareness are sadly lacking;

- Public education is critical, as the general population seldom comprehends the hazards of toxic substances;

- There should be a sense of urgency about all aspects of industrial safety, with special emphasis on 'worst-case possibilities', which should be incorporated into worker training, particularly in industrial plants with a high turnover of personnel;

- The parent company of a transnational corporation should carry out safety audits of its subsidiary plants in developing countries frequently, perhaps more often than it audits its plants at home;

- Sophisticated safety systems, often installed in industrialized nations, are imperative to compensate for lapses in the training of workers in Third World countries;

- Company executives should be technically and administratively trained in the processes for manufacturing toxic materials;

- Many parts of the Third World are growing rapidly without any zoning laws; suitable buffer zones should be established around potentially hazardous industrial plants;

- Cultural differences between foreign investors and host countries should be taken into account and preventive maintenance measures more thoroughly advocated;

- Host governments should closely monitor the operation and management of potentially hazardous industries, enforcing strict and timely sanctions for safety lapses; and

- When entering into agreements with transnational corporations, Third World governments should consider importing only those technologies that can be safely handled in the long run.

Bhopal is remembered as "the world's worst ever industrial disaster" at a time when industrial accidents are becoming increasingly common in industrializing countries. It demonstrated the potential negative impact of technology on the environment and human lives and the failure of government, business and science to work effectively together to protect people and their environment from industrial accidents.[39]

Perhaps the most important lesson is suggested by Dr. R. B. Sharma, Director of the Disaster Management Institute in Bhopal:

> *The basic point of disaster management recovery is the human dimension. We are too concerned with the material. There is little attention to what happens after the disaster.*[40]

Bhopal has underscored the need and importance of strict regulatory controls of international standards from the initial stages in the rapidly growing process of industrialization in a country. Bhopal also underscores the fact that enduring remedial efforts are needed to help people and communities fully recover in a number of dimensions: economic, social and physical and mental health.

This chapter has provided a sense of the grand dimensions of the disaster management challenge. Also it has illustrated the capabilities and capacities for disaster management in India today. In the following chapter, some conclusions and observations are suggested as India looks to meeting the future demands.

Endnotes

1. R. B. Sharma, Director, Disaster Management Institute, interview by authors, Bhopal, 24 September 1998.

2. Government Statement in reply to Rajya Sabha [Parliament, Council of States, Upper House], Unstarred Question No. 889, June 4 1998.

3. Indu Prakash, *Disaster Management: Societal Vulnerability to Natural Calamities and Man-Made Disasters, Preparedness and Response* (Ghaziabad: Rashtra Prahari Prakashan, 1994), 80.

4. Prakash, 81-3.

5. Prakash, 84-5.

6. *The Indian Express* (New Delhi), 9 September 1998.

7. *The Hindustan Times* (New Delhi), 8 September 1998.

8. *The Times of India* (New Delhi), 21 September 1998.

9. *The Hindustan Times* (New Delhi), 8 September 1998.

10. *India Today* (New Delhi), 21 September 1998, 26.

11. *The Hindustan Times* (New Delhi), 13 September 1998.

12. *India Today* (New Delhi), 21 September 1998, 29.

13. *The Hindustan Times* (New Delhi), 30 August 1998

14. *Newsweek*, 7 September 1998, 3.

15. Indu Prakash. This section is base on Dr. Prakash's description of drought, pages 92-103.

16. Prakash, 45-51.

17. Earthquake Rehabilitation Cell, Government of Maharashtra, *Maharashtra Emergency Earthquake Rehabilitation Program*, (Mumbai: July 1998), 1.

18. The *Times of India*(New Delhi), 16 June 1998. Also, *The Indian Express* (New Delhi), 17 June 1998.

19. *Outlook*, 6 July 1998.

20. *India Today* (New Delhi), 22 June 1998, 33. Also, *The Times* of India (New Delhi), 30 June 1998.

21. Bittu Sahgal, "Gujarat Cyclone: Ill Winds This Way Blow." *Times of India* (New Delhi), 30 June 1998.

22. *India Today* (New Delhi), 31 August 1998, 33.

23. *The Hindustan Times* (New Delhi), 28 August 1998.

24. Bharat Dogra, "When the Mountains Come Crashing Down," *The Times of India* (New Delhi), 26 August 1998.

25. S. M. A. Kazmi, "Danger: Landslide Zone," *The Indian Express* (New Delhi), 23 August 1998.

26. Om Prakash Kharbanda and E. A. Stallworthy, *Management Disasters and How to Prevent Them* (Aldershot: Gower Publications, 1986), 40.

27. R. B. Sharma, Director, Disaster Management Institute, interview by authors, Bhopal, 24 September 1998. See also *India*, (Australia: Lonely Planet, 1997), 772.

28. Paul Srivastava, *Bhopal: Anatomy of a Crisis* (Cambridge: Ballinger Publishing Company, n.d.), 48.

29. Srivastava, 49.

30. Srivastava, 53.

31. Srivastava, 57-7.

32. Anil Agarwal, Juliet Merifield and Rajesh Tandon, *No Place to Run: Local Realities and Global Issues of the Bhopal Disaster* (Highlander Centre and Society for Participatory Research in Asia, 1985), 3.

33. Ward Morehouse and M. Arun Subramaniam, *The Bhopal Tragedy: What Really Happened and What It Means for American workers and Communities at Risk, A Preliminary Report for the Citizens Commission on Bhopal,* 41.

34. Anil Agarwal, 3-4.

35. Larry Everest, *Behind the Poison Cloud: Union Carbide's Bhopal Massacre* (Chicago: Banner Press, n.d.), 156-7.

36. Government Reply to Lok Sabha, Unstarred Question No. 981, 2 June 1998.

37. Satinath Sarangi, Bhopal Peoples Health and Documentation Clinic, Sambhavna Trust, Bhopal, interview by authors at Sambhavna Clinic, 24 September 1998.

38. Martin Abraham, International Organization of Consumers Unions, *The Lessons of Bhopal: a Community Action Resource Manual on Hazardous Technologies* (IOCU, 1985), 14.

39. Martin Abraham, 1.

40. Sharma interview.

VIII. India's Disaster Management Environment

*The East bow'd low before the blast,In patient, deep disdain.
She let the legions thunder past,And plunged in thought again.* [1]

Matthew Arnold

The future for Indian disaster management is going to be more challenging than ever before. There is increasing awareness about the need to plan for disasters. Improved technology is available for warning and forecasting, and several positive steps have been initiated to reduce disasters. Yet the overall trend is towards more disaster-related deaths and losses. The reasons for this are:

- Continuing population growth which will overload the available infrastructure and services, even without the advent of disasters;

- Increasing pressure on a land that will have to feed the world's most populous nation but, year after year, is vulnerable to the vagaries of weather;

- Uneven economic growth that may result in a better life for some sectors while leaving others destitute and unable to ward off hazards;

- Technological advancement and attendant industrialization that, while offering the prospects for wondrous goods and services, also encourages conurbation and leaves the population vulnerable to natural and man-made disasters; and

- Interdependence of countries and regions whereby hazards in one region impact directly on others, such as low-land flooding caused by denudation of upland forests, or a nuclear accident in one region having fallout on another.

The Government of India has the requisite structure to cope with disasters. There are detailed orders and manuals on related subjects, particularly at the state level. But even now, the Central Government has yet to publish a national emergency management plan.

Experience shows that in the event of a disaster, the government response is generally tardy. This is primarily because bureaucracy, which was once considered the "steel frame" of administration, has over the years become inefficient and corrupt. The inefficiency itself is

149

a product of politicization of the services, which is having a very adverse effect on the morale and work culture of the officers. Besides, corruption has eaten into the vitals of the services. Things generally do not move without the speed money. The former Prime Minister, Rajiv Gandhi, is on record as having said that out of every rupee spent on development, only 25 paise (i.e. one-fourth of the sum) reached the common man; the rest was gobbled up by the intermediaries. The situation, if anything, is perhaps worse today. Millions are spent on flood protection schemes and drought relief measures, but only a fraction really shows.

Analyzing the disaster management in India, a commentator recently wrote:

"Lives are lost, families ruined and property is destroyed. The only survivors are those who govern: politicians, bureaucrats and their retinue. They go about their business of harassing citizens and feathering their nests. Nothing happens to them. A bureaucrat may be transferred or a politician harangued in public forums such as parliament, the state assemblies or commissions of inquiry. No one is ever brought to book. By implication, no one is held accountable for public safety. Thus, the very minimum requirement of governance is waived. Never mind disaster management, the government itself is the disaster." [2]

FALLING SHORT

The case studies of recent incidents show that India's current disaster management machinery has shortcomings, such as:

- Lackadaisical approach of authorities to tackling a disaster;
- Delayed response by the government officers;
- Absence of early warning systems;
- Lack of resources to undertake measures like mass evacuation;
- Inadequate coordination among the various departments;
- Non-existence and non-familiarization of standard operating procedures to be followed in providing disaster relief;
- Failure to keep essential stores like sand bags, medicines etc. in ready stock; and

150

- Inadequate coordination with the Army and other service organizations.

These shortcomings were blatantly exhibited during the recent 1998 floods in the country, when in the battered states of Assam, West Bengal, Bihar and Uttar Pradesh, over 2,000 people died, nearly eight million were rendered homeless and property worth Rs. 50 billion was damaged. A natural tragedy, as was rightly observed, has a "multiplier effect" when it is compounded by lack of vision and the refusal to learn from past mistakes."[3] Commenting on the landslides in the hill districts of Uttar Pradesh, when a batch of pilgrims inching in faith towards Hinduism's most sacred spot met a spine-chilling end, Bittu Sehgal deplored that warnings from the hill people and from the *Chipko Andolan* that these areas were geologically unstable and that the mountain chain was too fragile, were steadfastly ignored.[4] "Our trees have been stripped, our hill-folk have been victimized and our holy rivers have been defiled."[5]

The Orissa cyclone particularly exposed the weakness of the country's disaster management machinery. The civil administration virtually collapsed. Important district level functionaries deserted their posts. Relief money and material poured in from all parts of the country and abroad, but it could not be channeled to the affected areas or the needy people timely. There were also allegations of corruption. Dr. P.V. Unnikrishnan of the OXFAM, writing *After the Act of God* , commented that "it offers a classic, if numbing, case-study on the nexus between nature, poverty and criminally bad policy."

The one single factor which is upsetting the apple-cart of economic development in India and making it highly vulnerable to disasters is its galloping population. The number of urban agglomerations continue to increase. The civic amenities are not able to keep pace with the increasing urbanization. The gap between requirements and availability is getting widened. This disparity itself has in it the seeds of very grave disasters. The Indian Medical Association recently appealed to the Prime Minister to declare the population problem a "national emergency," saying that the National Family Planning Program had miserably failed in controlling the population. The Association identified three main factors responsible for the poor progress of family planning efforts: failure to eradicate illiteracy; the resultant gender bias; and the extreme centralization of the program resulting in a limited reach and lack of people's involvement. The Association expressed great concern over the fact that India would become the most populous country of the world by

2050 with a population of over 1,620 million. Its consequences on the quality of life, social harmony and the ecosystem will be disastrous.[6]

MOVING AHEAD

There are nevertheless some good beginnings. The National Center for Disaster Management, which was established by the Ministry of Agriculture, Government of India, has been conducting training programs on specific natural disasters like floods, earthquakes, droughts, cyclones, landslides, etc. for the senior and middle level government officers and NGOs working in the area of disaster management. The Center has initiated research and prepared case studies in the areas of disaster preparedness, mitigation, cost-benefit analysis of preparedness plans, environmental impacts of floods and drought, efficacy of organization structure, managing disasters in the states and the socio-psychological impacts of natural disasters. The Center is also preparing a database and documentation center within the Indian Institute of Public Administration, of which it is a part.

Similar institutes have come up at regional levels also. The Disaster Management Institute, Bhopal was set up in 1987 by the Government of Madhya Pradesh in the backdrop of the MIC gas leakage disaster. The Institute's primary goal is to evolve and enhance adequate competence for prevention, mitigation and management of disasters. It caters to the development of professional and managerial needs in government, public and private sectors in the field of management of natural and man-made disasters. The Centre for Disaster Management at the Yashada Government Training Institute in Pune, Maharashtra is a similar research and training institution which has assisted the state and districts with developing disaster management plans.

The World Bank, UN Development Program and DFID (Department for International Development, UK) are supporting different components of the Maharashtra state planning effort. The implementation strategy is based on a series of activities which provide support in the nature of infrastructure and organizational requirements. The activities include setting up of an Emergency Operations Center in the Mantralaya (State Government headquarters), District Control Rooms at all the district headquarters, a communication network comprising wireless (VHF) and satellite (VSAT) networks for the entire state, a computerized Disaster Management Information System, community disaster preparedness programs and training.

The Maharashtra state disaster planning effort provides a model for other states to follow. The objectives could be to:

- Assess the status of existing resources and facilities available with the various departments and agencies involved in disaster management in the state;

- Assess their adequacies in dealing with a disaster;

- Identify the requirements for institutional strengthening, technological support, up-gradation of information systems and data management for improving the quality of administrative response to disasters at the state level; and

- Make the state Disaster Management Plan an effective response mechanism as well as a policy and planning tool.

Natural disasters will continue to bedevil the country. It is important however that long term measures are thought of and implemented to prevent them as far as possible and, to the extent they are inevitable, face them in a planned and coordinated manner so as to reduce the pain and the trauma they bring in their wake. The Government of India should have a comprehensive National Disaster Management Plan. It would also be necessary, considering the country's geographical status, that appropriate coordination mechanisms are worked out with neighboring countries like Nepal and China. In the Malpa tragedy, that would have substantially cut down the delays in rescue operations caused by bad weather. It took almost three days for the government to get the requisite permission from Nepal to approach the landslide-hit area from that side of the border. All of this suggests an opportunity here to offer a summary and conclusions about India's disaster management process.

ASSESSING THE ENVIRONMENT

Having reviewed India's history of disasters, available services, government and private organizations, planning factors, and some examples of recent disaster events, it seem appropriate to offer a preliminary assessment of India's capability and capacity for disaster management. The review suggests some key questions about disaster planning and operations.

What is the strategic direction or doctrinal guidance provided to disaster planners and managers? The country lacks a formal framework for strategic guidance and doctrinal development. However, the confluence of effort by professionals associated with organizations such as the National Center for Disaster Management, Disaster Management Institute, Indira Gandhi National Open

University (IGNOU) and others has developed a professional body of knowledge relevant to India's environment. This is also reflected in professional books and journals, such as the *International Journal of Natural Disaster Reduction*, edited by M. C. Gupta and Vinod K. Sharma, under the aegis of the Indian Institute of Public Administration. The universal themes which have evolved from this effort suggest the following doctrinal imperatives for India's disaster management:

- Astrong focus on disaster prevention and mitigation;

- Long-term measures to fight earthquake–economic and technical effort;

- Control of economic development to reduce the impact on land and resulting changes to the flow of water run-off;

- Set aside funding by the states for disaster emergencies, augmented by Central Government grants;

- The need for networking among disaster management organizations, government agencies, and non-government, volunteer organizations;

- An emphasis on training and publication;

- Emphasis on the human dimension of disasters, particularly the social, medical, and psychological aspects of long-term recovery.

What is India's strategic plan and organization for disaster management? Except for an old regulation which dates to colonial times, the Central Government of India does not have a national emergency plan for disaster management. Under the Minister of Agriculture, the National Center for Disaster Management is now working on a National Disaster Management Plan. Given India's Constitutional guidelines of state responsibility for disaster management, and historical preference for devolving authority to regional levels of government, it seems unlikely that India will develop a Central Emergency Management Plan that provides more than policy guidance. It is further unlikely, given the states' role, that the Central Government will develop a national-level emergency management organization along the likes of the United States' Federal Emergency Management Agency (FEMA). The locus of disaster prevention and relief will remain at the state level.

154

Who is reponsible for providing disaster assistance in India and who does the work? Under the Constitution, responsibility rests primarily with the state governments. Few state governments have up-to-date and efficacious disaster management plans that are backed-up with in-place services and supplies. At the regional and local levels of government, the first responders are typically the staffs of the District Magistrate and the Superintendent of Police. The government workers that really do the lion's share of the work during disasters are government staff at district, sub-division, *tehsil* and village levels along with the police at district, sub-division and police station levels. This suggests where disaster assistance can best be applied by countries, International Organizations, and other volunteer organizations.

What is the role for NGOs in Indian disaster response? Disaster assistance is most effective in India with the intervention of non-government organizations. The larger NGOs typically have networks throughout out the country and, via coalition arrangements with other volunteer organizations, can extend their effort down to the lowest levels. Smaller, grassroots and volunteer organizations know the people, terrain and situation and are essential for focusing the effort. Thus, NGOs can bring outside resources to the disaster situation via an efficient network which ensures that supplies and services are applied where needed in a timely manner. The NGOs have also proven helpful in development programs which include training and mitigation activities.

How should International Organizations and Donor Nations provide assistance? India prefers not to request disaster assistance from donor nations or international organizations. Its stated policy is that the country will rely on its own resources to resolve disaster situations. International organizations and donor nations usually provide disaster assistance resources to local level governments and grass-roots organizations via on-site NGOs. The U.S. Agency for International Development, for example, provides assistance through the U.S. voluntary agencies, CARE and Catholic Relief Services, which are designated cooperating sponsors under the United States' PL 480 Title II Program.

Is there a common theme in India's disaster management planning and training? While disaster management professionals seek to effect rapid and effective response, there is great emphasis being placed on prevention through methods such as building safer structures, moving communities to safer locations, and educating people about disaster perils. There is an appreciation of the psychological dimension of the victims' struggle with disasters. There is also a universal interest in the requirements of long-term rehabilitation that exist well after the initial provision of food and shelter, such as counseling and medical care.

Are there additional lessons to be learned from the Bhopal disaster? The 1984 release of MIC gas at Bhopal has been well documented in articles and books describing the malfeasance of chemical plant managers and resulting disaster. As pointed out by a number of specialists, however, the long-term consequences continue well after the immediate damage and injuries have been controlled. This is clearly the case with Bhopal where people in the area of the Union Carbide plant continue to suffer from a range of serious health problems and where severe, enduring environmental damage may have taken place as well. Now, after 15 years have passed, there seems to be an important opportunity to help people while continuing research concerning the long-term effects of a chemical disaster upon a large population. There is a need to continue support to the victims of Bhopal, and there is important research to be done for those concerned with industrial and Weapons of Mass Destruction (WMD) terrorism incidents involving deadly chemicals in a populated area—and what long-term consequences should be anticipated.

How will India leverage new conceptual and technological advancements in the disaster management field? India's disaster management professionals are aware of the benefits of networking within Indian national domains and with international community. For example, the Disaster Management Institute at Bhopal and the National Center for Disaster Management in New Delhi have expressed an interest in developing cooperative relationships with other organizations around the globe to exchange information about training and research, and to facilitate disaster assistance operations. The country will be well-served by its active and open participation in international disaster management fora.

THE NUCLEAR SPECTER AND NATURAL DISASTERS

The nuclear dimension of disaster management made itself apparent in 1998 with the testing by India, and then Pakistan, of nuclear explosions (weapons). This seemed to boost the need for enhancing India's capabilities and capacities for disaster management as the possibility of a nuclear holocaust in the Indian sub-continent was predicted by several experts. In addition to facing an increasing number of natural disaster hazards, India now must contemplate the challenge caused by the release of the nuclear genie from the bottle.

Contentious issues remain unresolved between India and China. These are the Sino-Pak missile and nuclear collaboration, China claiming Arunachal Pradesh as part of its territory and holding on to Aksai Chin in the Ladakh area, incidents of Chinese incursions, and the issue of the Line of Actual Control.

Under siege by the current onslaught of cyclones, floods, earthquakes, and landslides described in previous chapters, nuclear weapons bring an added dimension to India's disaster management challenge that could be horrendous and overwhelming. The confrontation between India and Pakistan over the Jammu and Kashmir problem poses a proximate threat to peace and stability in the sub-continent. There were wars between the two countries in 1947, 1965 and 1971, and yet the problem remains unresolved. The acquisition of nuclear capability by both India and Pakistan has added a new and unwanted component to disaster prevention and assistance.

And yet, surprisingly, the Indians are not perturbed at the prospects. They have weathered invasions. They have suffered disasters. And therefore, while gearing up the existing mechanisms to face catastrophes which nature or man may inflict on them, they remain composed and phelegmatic because, as Lord Krishna says in *Bhagvad Gita*, He is the *Kala*, the eternal Time-spirit, the Destroyer of the worlds.

Kālo 'smi lokaksayakrtpravrddho
Lokānsamahartumiha pravrttah

(Chapter XI. Verse 32)

Endnotes

1. Matthew Arnold, "The East Bowed Low...," quoted in N. A. Palkhivala, *India's Priceless Heritage* (Bombay: Vidya Bhavan, 1994), 48.

2. Rajiv Desai, "Government is the Real Disaster," *The Sunday Times of India* (New Delhi: 30 August 1998).

3. "Fighting the Fury," *The Times of India* (New Delhi: 21 September 1998).

4. Chipko Andolan is a movement where the hill people embrace the trees to prevent their cutting.

5. Bittu Sehgal, "Nothing Divine About It," *The Sunday Times of India* (New Delhi: 30 August 1998).

6. The Indian Express (New Delhi: 13 July 1998).

Bibliography

Abraham, Martin. *The Lessons of Bhopal: A Community Action Resource Manual on Hazardous Technologies.* Penang, Malaysia: International Organisation of Consumers Unions, Regional Office for Asia and the Pacific, 1985.

Agarwal, Anil, Juliet Merrifield, and Rajesh Tandon. *No Place to Run : Local Realities and Global Issues of the Bhopal Disaster.* New Delhi: Highlander Centre and Society for Participatory Research in Asia, 1985.

Albala-Bertrand, J. M. *Political Economy of Large Natural Disasters*Oxford: Clarendon Press, 1993.

Alexander, David. *Natural Disasters.* London: UCL Press, 1993.

Anderson, Mary B., and Peter J. Wooddrow. *Rising from the Ashes: Development Strategies in Times of Disaster.* Paris: UNESCO, 1989.

Arya, A. S. *Action Plan for Earthquake Disaster Mitigation.* New Delhi: Indian Institute of Public Administration, 1994.

Asian Development Bank. *Disaster Mitigation in Asia and the Pacific.* Manila: 1991.

Atlas of Indian States. Chennai, India: TTK Pharma Limited, 1997.

Bagchi, Kathakali S. *Drought-Prone India: Problems and Prospectives* New Delhi: Agricole, 1991.

Banerjee, Brojendra Nath. *Bhopal Gas Tragedy : Accident or Experiment.* New Delhi: Paribus Publishers and Distributors, 1986.

Bapat, Arun, R. C.Kulkarni, and S. K. Guha. *Catalogue of Earthquakes in India and Neighbourhood from Historical Period up to 1979.* Roorkee: Indian Society of Earthquake Technology, 1983.

Baranwal, Jayant, ed. *SP's Military Yearbook .* New Delhi: Guide Publications, 1997.

Basu, Sreelekha. "Floods and Water Management." *Yojana* 29, nos. 6, 7 (1-16 April 1985): 13-17, 31-2.

Bhandare, S. S. and J. K. Mukhopadhyay, eds. *Statistical Outline of India, 1997-98.* Mumbai: Tata Services Limited, 1997.

Bhatia, B.M. *Famines in India : A Study in Some Aspects of the Economic History of India (1860-1965).* Bombay: Asia Publishing House, 1967.

Bhatt, Chandiprasad. *Impact of Natural Disasters on Environment and Development: Examples from Himalaya and Eastern and Western Ghats.* New Delhi: Indian Institute of Public Administration, 1994.

Bogard, William. *The Bhopal Tragedy : Language, Logic, and Politics in the Production of a Hazard.* Boulder: Westview Press, 1989.

Carter, W. Nick. *Disaster Management: A Disaster Manager's Handbook.* Manila: Asian Development Bank, 1991.

Chishti, Anees. *Dateline Bhopal.* New Delhi: Concept Publishing House, 1986.

Chitkara, M.G. ed., *Encyclopaedia of Ecology, Environment and* Pollution. New Delhi: A. P. H. Publishing Corporation, 1998.

Council for Advancement of People's Action and Rural Technology (CAPART). *Disaster Preparedness - A Handbook for Trainers* . New Delhi: CAPART, Ministry of Rural Development, n.d.

_____. *Strengthening of Community Participation and Role of NGOs.* New Delhi: CAPART, Ministry of Rural Development, 1995.

Court, Thijs de la. *Different Worlds: Development Cooperation Beyond the Nineties.* Translated by Lin Pugh. Utrecht, The Netherlands: International Books, 1992.

Das, Pradip Kumar, and Parag Phukan. *Earthquakes and Volcanoes.* New Delhi: Indus Publishing Company, 1994.

Disaster Management Institute (DMI). *Characterization & Management of Hazardous Wastes* . Bhopal, India: DMI, Housing & Environment Department, Government of Madhya Pradesh, August 1997.

_____. *Chemical Accidents, Causes, Prevention & Management* Bhopal, India: DMI, September 1998.

_____. *Earthquake Disaster Management, A Base Document* . Bhopal, India: DMI, October 1996.

_____. *Earthquake Disaster Management, Selected Readings* . Bhopal, India: DMI, August 1998.

_____. *Flood Disaster Management.* Bhopal, India: July 1997.

_____. *Industrial Safety and Law.* Bhopal, India: DMI, August 1996.

_____. *Management of Chemical Accident.* Bhopal, India: DMI, August 1998.

162

_____. *Management of Chemical Accident, Refresher Course for Top Executive*. Bhopal, India: DMI, February 1995.

_____. *Regulatory Provisions & Laws Pertaining to Environment Safety & Occupational Health*. Bhopal, India: DMI, June 1997.

Dreze, Jean and Amartya Sen. *India, Economic Development and Social Opportunity*. Delhi: Oxford University Press, 1998.

Dubhashi, PR. "Drought and Development." *Economic and Political Weekly* 27, no.13, (28 March 1992): 1727-36.

Economic Division, Ministry of Finance. *Economic Survey 1997-98*. New Delhi: Government of India, 1998.

Everest, Larry. *Behind the Poison Cloud : Union Carbide's Bhopal Massacre*. Chicago: Banner Press, 1986.

Gautam, Ashutosh. *Earthquake: A Natural Disaster*. New Delhi: Ashish, 1994.

Green, Stephen. *International Disaster Relief: Toward a Responsive System*. New York: McGraw Hill, 1977.

Gupta, Sharad. *Vulnerability Atlas of India* . New Delhi: Government of India, Ministry of Urban Development, Building Materials and Technology Promotion Council, 1997.

Hemmady, A.K.R. *Earthquakes*. New Delhi: National Book Trust, 1996.

Home Office. *Dealing with Disaster*. London: HMSO, 1994.

Indian Institute of Public Administration. *Annual Report, 1997-98*. New Delhi: IIPA, 1998.

Indian Ministry of Planning and Programme Implementation, Central Statistical Organisation, Department of Statistics. *Statistical Abstract India 1997*, 2 Vols. New Delhi: December 1997.

International Federation of Red Cross and Red Crescent Societies. *World Disasters Report 1998*. Oxford: Oxford University Press, 1998.

Kharbanda, O. P. and E. A.Stallworthy. *Management Disasters : And How to Prevent Them*. Aldershot: Gower Publications, 1986.

International Federation of Red Cross and Red Crescent Societies. *World Disasters Report, 1998*. Oxford, GB: Oxford University Press, 1998.

Kouach, Edward L. *Earth's Fury : An Introduction to Natural Hazards and Disaster*. Old Tappan: Prentice Hall, 1995.

Kundu, Apurba. *Militarism in India, the Army and Civil Society in Consensus* New Delhi: Viva Books, 1998.

Maharashtra [State] Government. *Maharashtra Emergency Earthquake Rehabilitation Programme* : *An International Workshop on Disaster Management Plan for the State of Maharashtra.* Mumbai use: 1998.

Maharashtra [State] Government. *Maharashtra Disaster Management Plan : Risk Assessment and Vulnerability Analysis.* Mumbai use: 1998.

Maharashtra [State] Government. *Risk Assessment and Vulnerability Analysis, Maharashtra Disaster Management Plan* Mumbai: July 1998.

Mandal, G. S. *Natural Disasters.* New Delhi: Indian Institute of Public Administration, 1994.

Marwah, Ved. *Uncivil Wars, Pathology of Terrorism in India*. New Delhi: Harper Collins, 1997.

Mathur, S.M. *Physical Geology of India.* New Delhi: National Book Trust, 1991.

Merriman, P. A. and C. W. A. Browitt. *Natural Disasters: Protecting Vulnerable Communities.* London: Thomas, 1993.

Middleton, Neil and Phil O'Keefe. *Disaster and Development: The Politics of Humanitarian Aid.* London: Pluto Press, 1998.

Ministry of Environment and Forests. *Guidelines for Management and Handling of Hazardous Wastes* New Delhi: Government of India, 1991.

Ministry of Health and Family Welfare. *Annual Report, 1997-98.* New Delhi: Government of India, 1998.

Ministry of Information and Broadcasting. *India 1998, A Reference Manual.* New Delhi: Government of India, 1998.

Misra, Girish K, and G. C. Mathur., eds. *Natural Disaster Reduction.* New Delhi: Reliance Publishing House 1993.

Modi, Jatin. "Disaster Management." *Quarterly Journal of the All-India Institute of Local Self-Government*, 10, no. 3 (Jul-Sep 1989): 133.

Morton, Ron L. *Music of the Earth: Volcanoes, Earthquakes and other Geological Wonders.* New York: Plenum Press, 1996.

Naidu, Raghavulu B. *Disaster Management.* Tirupati: Sri Venkateswara University, 1984.

Narasimhan, B. "Natural Disaster Management: Current Concerns." *ASCI Journal of Management*, 24. no. 2 (March 1995): 112-119.

Padmanabhan, B.S. "Disaster Management and Development." *Yojana* 36, no. 22 (15 December 1992): 15-16.

National Centre for Disaster Management. *India - Disaster Management Training Country Workshop.* New Delhi: Indian Institute of Public Administration, 1993.

Paranjape, H. K. "The Bhopal Gas Disaster. A Chronology of Principal Events in the Bhopal Gas Disaster Litigation." *Janata* 46, no. 34 (1 December 1991): 9-11.

Planning Commission. *Approach Paper to the Ninth Five Year Plan (1997-2002).* New Delhi: Government of India, 1996.

Prakash, Indu. *Disaster Management: Societal Vulnerability to Natural Calamities and Manmade Disasters, Preparedness and Response.* Ghaziabad: Rashtra Prahari Prakashan, 1994.

Prasad, Kamta and B. D.Singh. *Drought Disaster and Development.* New Delhi: Mittal, 1994.

Proceedings of Sixth World Conference on Earthquake Engineering Meerut: Sarita Prakashan, 1977.

Proceedings of the Symposium on Earthquake Disaster Mitigation. Roorkee: University of Roorkee, 1981.

Rajan, K. *Natural Disaster Management in National Development: An Indian Perspective.* New Delhi: Indian Institute of Public Administration, 1994.

Ramesh, K. S. *Cyclone Disaster Management in Coastal District of Andhra Pradesh : A Case Study* . New Delhi: Indian Institute of Public Administration, 1994.

Rayalaseema Geographical Society. *All India Symposium on Drought Prone Areas of India.* Tirupati: Sri Venkateshwar University, 1979.

Sahabat Alam (Friends of the Earth). *Bhopal Tragedy - One Year After.* Penang, Malaysia: Friends of the Earth, 1986.

Sahay, S. "Bhopal: The Shocking Verdict." *Mainstream* 27, no. 22 (25 February 1989): 39.

Satpute, Shaila. "The Latur Earthquake." *Manushi* 78 (September-October 1993): 18-20.

Sayee Kumar, V and S. Gopala Krishnan. "Disaster Management : A Psychosocial Crisis." *Social Welfare* 36, no. 5 (August 1989): 33-34.

Sharma, Sanjay, and Yatish Mishra. *Kashmir Tourism to Terrorism.* Delhi: Sane Publications, 1995.

Sharma, Vinod K, ed. *Disaster Management.* National Centre for Disaster Management, Indian Institute of Public Administration, New Delhi use: 1997.

_____. *Training of Trainers Programme on Disaster Management for NGOs.* New Delhi: National Centre for Disaster Management, Indian Institute of Public Administration, 1997.

_____. Training Program on Flood and Landslides Management. New Delhi: National Centre for Disaster Management, Indian Institute of Public Administration, 1997.

Sharma, Vinod K., and J. N. Upadhyay. *Training of Trainers Programme on Drought Management .* New Delhi: National Centre for Disaster Management, Indian Institute of Public Administration, n.d.

Shastri, Lalit. *Bhopal Disaster.* New Delhi: Criterion Publications, 1985.

Shrivastava, Paul. *Bhopal: Anatomy of a Crisis.* London: Paul Cahpman Publishers, 1992.

_____. *Managing Industrial Crises : Lessons of Bhopal.* New Delhi: Vision Books, 1987.

Silveira, D. M. *India Book.* Bombay: Classic, 1998.

Singh, Shailendra K., Subhash C. Kundu, and Shobha Singh. *Disaster Management.* New Delhi: Mittal, 1998.

Singh, R. K. Jasbir, ed. *Indian Defense Year Book, 1998-99 .* Dehra Dun, India: 1998.

Sinha, P.C., ed. *Encyclopaedia of Disaster Management.* New Delhi: Anmol Publications Pvt. Ltd., 1998.

Smith, Keith. *Environmental Hazards: Assessing Risk and Reducing Disaster.* London: Routledge, 1996.

Smith, Philip B., Samuel E. Okoye, Jaap de Wilde, and Priya Deshingkar. *The World at the Crossroads :Towards a Sustainable, Equitable and Livable World, A Report to the Pugwash Council .* London: Earthscan Publications Ltd, 1994.

"Special Issue on Crisis and Disaster Management." *Asian Review of Public Administration* 2, no. 1-2 (Jan-Dec 1990): 1-122.

Sudan, Randeep. "Disasters Management : Administrative Response to Cyclones." *Indian Journal of Public Administration* 38, no. 1 (Jan-Mar 1992): 37-49.

Thapliyal, G.B., *A Case Study of Earthquake Disaster in Uttarkashi : Response to Crisis.* New Delhi: Indian Institute of Public Administration, 1998.

Toft, B., and S. Reynolds. *Learning from Disasters: A Management Approach.* Woburn: Butterworth Heinemaun, 1995.

Thomas, Bryn, et al. *India.* Hawthorn, Australia: Lonely Planet, November 1997.

Turner, Barry A. and Nick F. Pidgeon. *Man-made Disasters.* Oxford: Butterworth-Heinemann, 1997.

U.S. Agency for International Development. *U.S. Mission to India Disaster Relief Plan.* New Delhi: USAID, 9 March 1998.

United Nations Centre for Human Settlements (Habitat). *Human Settlements and Natural Disasters.* New York: U.N. 1989.

Verma, B. K. *Disaster Management in India: A Community Perspective.* New Delhi: Indian Institute of Public Administration, 1994.

Vivek, P. S. *The Struggle of Man against Power : Revelation of 1984 Bhopal Tragedy.* Delhi: Himalaya Publishing House, 1990.

Weir, David. *The Bhopal Syndrome: Pesticides, Environment, and Health .* San Francisco: Sierra Club Books, 1987.

Weirsing, Klaus. *Basic Principles and Elements of Disaster Mitigation.* New Delhi: Indian Institute of Public Administration, 1994.

Zmolek, Mike. "Aid Agencies, NGOs and Institutionalisation of Famine." *Economic and Political Weekly* 25, no. 1 (6 January 1990): 37-48.

Annex

NGOS in India

Some of the important NGOs working in the field of Disaster Management are listed here to assist disaster management planners.

Andhra Pradesh

Name:	*Social Educational and Economic Development Society (SEEDS)*
Address:	16/2, Arundlpet, Guntur, Andhra Pradesh - 522002
Phone:	0863-351631
Fax:	0863-351481
Area of interest:	Flood, Cyclone, Drought management.

Name:	*Association for Social and Humanize Action (ASHA)*
Address:	Mothuguden, Khammam, Andhra Pradesh -507113
Area of interest:	Flood management.

Name:	*ACTION (Association for Rural and Tribal Development)*
Address:	'Krishna Sadan' Dr. Meda Ranga Prasada Rao Garden, Post-Hukumpet, Rajahmundry, Andhra Pradesh-533103
Phone:	61442
Area of interest:	Flood, Cyclone management.

Assam

Name:	*Katigorah Gram Unnayan Parishad*
Address:	Post - Behara IV, Cachar, Assam - 788817
Area of interest:	Flood, Cyclone management.

Bihar

Name:	*Gramin Vikas Parisar*
Address:	At & PO. Andhra, Madhubani, Bihar - 847401
Phone:	06273-73238
Area of interest:	Flood, Drought management.

Bahir *(continued)*

Name:	*Lok Jagriti Kendra*
Address:	Madhupur, Deoghar, Bihar - 815353
Phone:	06438-24562
Area of interest:	Drought management.

Chandigarh

Name:	*S.S.Memorial Educational Society*
Address:	3495/40 D, Chamkaur Sahib, Chandigarh - 140112
Phone:	694465
Area of interest:	Flood management.

Gujarat

Name:	*Abhikram*
Address:	Gujarat Lok Samiti Premises, Lal Darwaja, Ahmedabad, Gujarat 380001
Phone:	5507296, 7483099
Fax:	6613807
Area of interest:	Watershed development and conservation, deepening of wells.

Name:	*World Vision*
Address:	Sahitya Seva Sadan, Gujarat College Cross Road, Ellisbridge, Ahmedabad-380006
Phone:	079-463452/7410247
Area of interest:	Disaster relief.

Haryana

Name:	*Youth Action for Rural Development*
Address:	290, MIG, Housing Board Colony, Karnal, Haryana-132001
Phone:	0184-251290
Fax:	0184-253494
Area of interest:	Flood relief.

Himachal Pradesh

Name:	*People's Action for People in Need (PAPN)*
Address:	Village & Post - Andheri, Via-Sangraha, Sirmour
	Himachal Pradesh-173023
Phone:	01702-8158
Area of interest:	Mobilization of volunteers for emergency relief work during natural disasters.

Karnataka

Name:	*Asian Institute for Rural Development*
Address:	No. 7/A, Ratnavilasa Road, Basavangudi, BangaloreKarnataka - 560004
Phone:	080-6604091
Fax:	080-6604091
Area of interest:	Publication of news-items on disaster management in the monthly 'AIRD news'.

Kerala

Name:	*International Center for Study and Development (ICSD)*
Address:	P.O. Valakom, Post Bag no.1, Kollam, Kerala - 691532
Phone:	047570-2359, 2075, 2008
Fax:	047570-2359
Area of interest:	Awareness / Support to relief work.

Name:	*Agency for Development of Rural Resources and Technology.*
Address:	DART, Post-Kodukulanji, Kerala -689508
Phone:	0479-352230
Area of interest:	Conservation and development of rural resources and technology to avoid natural calamities.

Madhya Pradesh

Name:	**Disaster Management Institute**
Address:	Paryavaran Parisar, E-5, P.B. No. 563
	Arera Colony, Bhopal 462016

Madhya Pradesh *(continued)*

Phone:	0755 566715; 561538
Fax:	0755 566653
Email:	dmibpl@bom6.vsnl.net.in
Area of Interest:	Training, Research, Technical consultation.

Maharashtra

Name:	**Bhartiya Jeevan Vikas Pratishthan**
Address:	Siddhrath Nagar, Teka, Nagpur, Maharashtra-440017
Area of interest:	Earthquake.

Name:	*Ecumenical Development Center of India*
Address:	Ghani Manzil, Chhaoni, Katol Road, Nagpur, Maharashtra - 440013
Phone:	0712-525786
Fax:	0712-525786
Area of interest:	Awareness and educational programs for volunteers.

New Delhi

Name:	*CARE India*
Address:	B-28, Greater Kailash-I, PO Box 4220,New Delhi-110048
Phone:	6221728, 6418422
Fax:	6483007, 6473098
Email:	CARE.IN@cared.ernet.in
Area of interest:	Relief in humanitarian crises, achieving sustainable development.

Name:	**CASA, Church's Auxiliary for Social Action**
Address:	Rachna Building, 2 Rajendra Place Pusa Road New Delhi-110008
Phone:	5761597; 5767231, 5715498; 5715538
Fax:	575 2502
Email:	casard@axcess.net.in

Name:	*Catholic Relief Services*
Address:	Vishal Market, 4,5,6, Bhai Parmanand Colony Shopping Center Mukherjee Nagar West, G.T.B. Nagar P. O. Delhi 110009
Phone:	745 0590; 745 0577
Fax:	
E-mail:	
Area of interest:	Humanitarian assistance, community development

Name:	*The Indian Red Cross*
Address:	No. 1, Red Cross Road, New Delhi 110 001
Phone:	91 11 371 6441/6424
Fax:	91 11 371 7454
E-mail:	indcross@nde.vsnl.net.in
Area of interest:	Disaster relief, humanitarian assistance.

Name:	*Oxfam (India) Trust*
Address:	B-3, Geethanjali Enclave, New Delhi- 110017
Phone:	011-6857075
Fax:	011-6186646
E-mail:	oxfam@oxim.unv.ernet.in
Area of interest:	Emergency relief in times of crisis, long-term sustainable development.

Name:	*ACTIONAID*
Address:	E-270, Greater Kailash - II, New Delhi.
Phone:	6418885/6/7
Fax:	6233525
E-mail:	vandanaj@actionaid.india.org
Area of interest:	Emergency relief.

Name:	*Genesis Foundation*
Address:	A1/265 Safdarjung Enclave, New Delhi.
Phone:	6178082/6193537
E-mail:	Rexgenesis@softhame.net
Area of interest:	Disaster relief.

New Delhi *(continued)*

Name:	*National Council of YMCAs of India*
Address:	Post Box No.-14, Bharatt Yuvak Bhawan, Jai Singh Road, New Delhi - 110001
Phone:	011-3360769
Fax:	011-334285
Area of interest:	Organizing emergency relief and rehabilitation

Name:	*Voluntary Health Association of India*
Address:	40 Institutional Area, Behind Qutab Hotel, New Delhi 110016
Phone:	651 8071; 651 8072
Fax:	
E-mail:	
Area of interest:	Public health services; interest in disaster assistance

Orissa

Name:	*Association for Social Action and Rural Development (ASARD)*
Address:	At & PO. Raikia, Phulbani, Orissa - 762101
Area of interest:	Flood management.

Name:	*Jeevan Bikash*
Address:	At-Gopinathpur, PO. Lendo, Via-Nirakarpur, Khurda, Orissa-752019
Area of interest:	Training and awareness in disaster management.

Name:	*Pragati*
Address:	Post Box No. 32, Puri, Orissa - 752001
Phone:	06752-24813
Area of interest:	Training in disaster management.

Name:	**National Institute for Sustainable Tropical Agriculture & Human Action (NISTHAA)**
Address:	2081, Chintamaniswar, Bhubaneswar, Orissa-751006
Phone:	0674-415655
Area of interest:	Flood, Drought management.

174

Punjab

Name:	*Punjab Action Group for Rural Development (PARUD)*
Address:	218, Guru Hargobind Nagar, Phagwara, Punjab.
Phone:	01824-63394
Fax:	01824-61760
Area of interest:	Rural Development and Environment.

Rajasthan

Name:	**Society for Sustainable Development**
Address:	Shah Inayat Khirkiya, Karauli, Rajasthan.
Phone:	07464-20065
Fax:	07464-20948 (PP)
Area of interest:	Flood, Drought management.

Tamilnadu

Name:	**Ryan Foundation International**
Address:	Westy Mada St. Srinagar Colony, Madras, Tamilnadu-600015
Phone:	0144-2351993
Fax:	0144-4910746
Area of interest:	Providing food, fuel, water, shelter and employment.

Name:	**Gramalaya**
Address:	31-A/29, Nesavalan Colony, Salai road, Worius, Tiruchi, Tamilnadu-620003
Phone:	0431-761263
Area of interest:	Flood, Drought management.

Name:	*TRUPA*
Address:	PO. Sirukudalpatty, Taluk-Tirupputur, PMT, Tamilnadu-630215
Area of interest:	Drought management.

Tamilnadu *(continued)*

Name:	**Vivekananda Kendra.**
Address:	Vivekananda Puram, Kanyakumari, Tamilnadu-629702
Phone:	04653-71232, 71296
Fax:	04653-71296
Area of interest:	Low cost house construction and economic activities based on resources locally available.

Name:	*Social Action Movement (SAM)*
Address:	Mamandur, GST Road, Chengai MGR, Tamilnadu.
Phone:	04115-75215
Fax:	04115-75215
Area of interest:	Drought relief, fire accident management.

Name:	**Rural Institute for Development Education.**
Address:	45, Periyar Nagar, Little Kanchipuram, Tamilnadu-631503
Phone:	24223
Fax:	23599
Area of interest:	Training and construction work.

Uttar Pradesh

Name:	*Himalayan Action Research Center (HARC)*
Address:	744, Indiranagar Phase-II, PO. New Forest, Dehradun, Uttar Pradesh - 248006
Phone :	620121
Area of interest:	Earthquake

Name:	*Center for Research on Ecology, Environment Application, Training and Education.*
Address:	91/2, Vijay Park, Dehradun, UP.
Phone:	0135-623437, 625495
Fax:	0135-623437
Area of interest:	Ecological principles of disaster management.

176

Uttar Pradesh *(continued)*

Name:	***Samanvaya (Federation of Hill NGOs of Uttarakhand)***
Address:	R.No.2, Himalaya Hotel, Gandhi Chowk, Ranikhet, Almora, UP -263648
Phone:	05966-2806
Fax:	05966-2451
Area of interest:	Disaster mitigation training and earthquake resistant construction.

Name:	**Lok Chetna Manch**
Address:	"Pravas," Sheetala Puri, Village & PO.-Ranibagh, Nainital, UP -263126
Phone:	05946-22361
Area of interest:	General awareness about disaster management.

Name:	***Sahyog***
Address:	C-179/298, Pandey Bhawan, Betia Hata, Shivpuri, Gorakhpur, U.P.
Phone:	0551-339774
Fax:	0551-339774
Area of interest:	Flood management.

Name:	***People's Action for National Integration (PANI)***
Address:	At / PO. Chachikpur, Via-Goshainganj,Ambedkar Nagar, Faizabad, UP - 224141
Area of interest:	Medical relief and food for work.

West Bengal

Name:	***Tarun Sangha***
Address:	Village and Post Biswas, Midnapore, West Bengal - 721636
Phone:	03228-66174, 66729
Area of interest:	Flood and Cyclone relief, and rehabilitation work.

Name:	***Vivekananda Adibasi Kalyan Samiti***
Address:	Village and Post. Chamtagara, Bankura, West Bengal-722137
Phone:	03242-74202
Area of interest:	Drought management.

Index

A

Agricultural drought 28

Agriculture xiii, 2, 23, 51, 90-93, 100, 103-104, 113-114, 125, 127, 152, 174

All India Radio 37, 58, 140

Air Force 63, 79, 84, 121-123, 132

Ajit Singh Bains 5, 122

Arabian Sea 35, 37, 43, 45

Army ii-iii, ix, xi, 6, 8, 26, 62, 79-81, 83-85, 87, 121-123, 128-129, 132-133, 140, 150, 164

Army Areas ix

Army Field Formations 79

Army Organization ix, 80

Assam iii, v-6, 17, 23-24, 32-33, 49, 77-78, 110, 119, 122, 124, 150, 169

Assam Rifles 77-78

Avalanches 39

Average Annual Temperature ix, 46

B

Baguios 35

Balasore 124

Barak 45

Bay of Bengal 35, 37, 39, 43, 45

Bhakra Beas Management Board 6, 121

Bhatwari 127

Bhopal v, viii-ix, xiii, 9, 14, 18, 32, 41-42, 87, 97-98, 104,
111, 117, 119, 134-137, 139-147, 152, 155-156, 161-163,
165-167, 171

Bihar v-6, 17, 23-24, 32, 45, 50, 54, 60, 108, 110, 117, 119,
123-124, 150, 169-170

Border Roads Development Board 56

Border Security Force 6, 8, 77-78, 121-122, 133

C

Cabinet Committee 2, 90, 93, 125

CARE-India xiii, 4, 107-108, 115

Cabinet Committee on Drought 125

Central Crisis Group 94

Central Health Education Bureau 73

Central Industrial Security Force 77-78

Central Relief Commissioner 91, 93

Central Reserve Police Force 77-78

Central Water and Power Commission 24

China 15, 13, 35, 44, 47, 62-63, 74, 78, 124, 153, 156

Civil Aviation 57

Civil Defense vii, 27, 73-74

Coast Guard 79-80

Commissioner for Railway Safety 54

Communication 26, 58, 73, 83, 127

Complex Disasters 15

Compound Disasters 15

Contingency Action Plan 91-92, 103

Control Room 3, 26, 92, 96, 99, 128

Conurbation 15-16

Coastal Protection and Development Advisory Committee 7, 131

Calamity Relief Fund 100

Crisis Management Group 3, 5, 93, 96, 121

Crops 23

Cyclone Warning Centers 37

Cyclone Distress Mitigation Committees 38

cyclones 11, 14, 16-17, 23, 35, 37-38

Cyclones vii, 7, 23, 37, 167

D

Damodar Valley Corporation 64

Darbhanga 6, 54, 123

Deputy Collector 3, 99

Director General of Civil Defense 73

Directorate General of Civil Aviation 57

Directorate General of Health Services 72

Disaster Assistance 108

Disaster Management Plan 97, 153, 164

District Control Room 99, 152

District Level vii

District Magistrate 3-4, 11, 79, 85, 88, 99, 111, 114, 139, 154

District Relief Committee 4, 99

Disaster Management Institute xiii, 9, 32, 97, 144, 152, 156, 162

Donor Countries viii

Doordarshan 37, 58, 68

Droughts vii,16

Dunda 127

E

Early Warning 18

Earthquake vii-ix, 15, 9, 14, 16-17, 21, 32, 34-35, 41-42, 87, 89, 98, 128, 145, 161-165, 167, 172, 176

Earthquake Examples ix, 32

Earthquakes vii, 15, 9, 16-17, 32, 42, 161-164

East India Company 29

El Niño 28

Emergency Operations Center 3, 92, 96

Emergency Phase 18

Everest, Larry 163

Exclusion Zone 61

F

Family Planning Program 48, 151

Famine Codes 29

Famine Commission 29

Famine Relief Codes 30

Famines vii, 29, 41, 161

Financial Arrangements vii

Fire Fighting vii

Five Year Plans 27, 31

Flood Relief Society 5, 122

Floods vii, 15, 5, 16, 23, 25-26, 119, 161

Foreign Military Studies ii-iii

G

Garo Hills 124

Geography vii, 43

Geology vii, 43, 164

Godavari 45, 56

Government ii-iii, 2, 5, 7-8, 10-11, 19, 21-22, 24, 26, 29, 31, 38-39, 41

Gujarat v, ix, 4-5, 7, 17, 23-25, 35-37, 56-57, 60, 63, 107, 110, 115, 117, 119, 129-131, 146, 170

Gurdaspur 5, 120-121

H

Haryana v, 5, 17, 23-24, 110, 120, 122, 170

Hazardous Substances Management 94

Health xiii, 13, 67, 72-73, 87, 98, 103, 108-109, 111, 127, 142, 147, 163-164, 167, 174

Himachal v, 5, 17, 33, 60, 120-122, 171

Himalayas 32, 39, 43, 45-47, 121, 124

Home Guard vii, 27, 74, 87

Home Guards vii, 74, 87

Hospitals 71

Humanitarian ii, xi, xiii, 13, 21, 41

Hybrid Disasters 14

Hydrological drought 27

I

Indian disaster 149

International Decade for Natural Disaster Reduction 21, 112

India Meteorological Department 35, 37, 90-91

India Meteorological Department 26, 35, 37, 42, 90-91

Indira Gandhi 10

Industrial and Technological Hazards 15

Infrastructure vii, 43, 50

International Organizations 105, 112, 155

Indo-Tibetan Border Police 77-78, 84, 129, 132-133

J

Jabalpur 128

Jawahar Lal Institute 72

Jharsuguda 124

K

Kandla Port 7, 36, 129-131

Kapurthala 5, 120

Kashmir iii, v, 5, 11, 17, 32, 49, 55, 62, 67, 78, 110, 119-120, 157, 166

Katihar 6, 123

Kaziranga National Park 122

Killari 127

Kosi River 24

Krishna 45, 56, 166, 169

L

Landslides 5, 8, 16, 39, 41, 119, 132-133, 166

Latur 84, 127-128, 165

M

Macchu Floods 25

Madhubani 123, 169

Maharashtra State Government 16

Managing Disasters vii

Man-made Disasters 167

Master of Arts iii

Medha Patkar 65

Medical Stores Organization 71

Meghalaya v-6, 17, 124

Minister of Agriculture 2, 19, 94, 154

Ministry of Environment and Forests 94, 142,164

Ministry of Home Affairs 55, 73-74, 93

Ministry of Surface Transport 52

Mitigation 18, 34, 38, 41, 97, 161, 165, 167

Mohammed Bin Tughlaq 28

Monghyr 123

N

Narmada Bachao Andolan 65

National Calamity Relief Committee 100

National Center xiii, 2, 10, 19, 22

National Center for Disaster Management xiii, 2, 10, 19, 22, 94, 103, 113-114, 151, 153-154, 156

National Civil Defense College 74

National Crisis Management Committee 91, 93

National Development Council 100

National Disaster Management Plan 2, 11, 19, 95, 114, 153-154

National Environmental Engineering and Research Institute 73

National Fire Service College 73

National Institute of Communicable Diseases 72

National Power Grid 60

National Security Guard 77-78

National Telecom Policy 59

Natural Calamities Committee 38

Natural Disasters viii, 14, 161-162, 164, 167

National Center for Disaster Management xiii, 94, 103, 113-114, 154, 156

National Fund for Calamity Relief 100

NGOS 169

National Thermal Power Corporation 60

Nuclear Specter viii

Nuclear Weapons 60-61

O

Orissa v, 5-8, 17, 23-24, 35-38, 54, 57, 60, 95, 108, 110, 117, 119, 124, 131-132, 151, 174

Osmanabad 127-128

P

Pradeshik Armed Constabulary 8, 133

Pakistan 11, 37, 44, 47, 62-63, 78, 156-157

Paramilitary Forces vii, ix, 77

Patel 3, 73, 99

Patwari 3, 99

Public Distribution System 30

Police iii, vii, ix, 8, 26, 75-78, 84, 87, 111, 128-129, 132-133, 154

Population v, vii, ix, 24, 47, 49, 55, 64

Population Growth ix, 49

Power 24, 59-60, 167

Power Grid Corporation of India 60

Pradesh v, 5-6, 8, 17, 23-24, 33, 35-38, 42, 50, 57, 60, 62, 74, 78, 97, 103, 108, 110, 117, 119-122, 124, 128, 132-133, 141, 152, 156, 162, 165, 169, 171-172

Pre-disaster Phase 18

Preparedness 18, 26, 103, 108, 125, 141, 145, 162, 165

Prevention xi, xiii, 18, 162

Prime Minister 2

Public Health vii, 72, 87

Punjab iii, v, 5, 17, 23, 25, 54, 58, 110, 120, 122, 175

Purnea 123

R

Railways 52

Ramakrishna Mission 107

Reconstruction 19, 106

Rehabilitation 19, 21, 109, 128, 145, 164

Relief vii, ix, xiii, 2-5, 18, 30, 38, 67-68, 72, 74, 83, 87-88, 91-94, 96, 99-100, 104, 107-110, 113-114, 116-117, 121-123, 127, 131, 151, 155, 163, 167, 172-173

Response xi, 18, 90, 97, 103, 115, 125, 139, 141, 145, 165, 167

Risk Assessment and Vulnerability Analysis 16, 21-22, 164

Rivers 56, 128

Roads 54, 56, 83-84, 121, 129

S

Saharsa 123

Samastipur 123

Sambalpur 124

Sambhavna Trust xiii, 111, 142, 147

Sanitation 106

Sardar Patel Institute of Public Administration 73

Scarcity Relief Division ix, 91-92

State Crisis Management Group 3, 96

Shipping and Ports 56

Sinha, P.C. 166

Slow Onset Hazards 15

Social Welfare Board 26

South Oscillation 28

Special River Commissions 26

State Level vii

State Police Organization ix

Static Formations 79, 85

Strategic Plan iii, 108

Sudden Onset Hazards 15

T

Tamilnadu v, 17, 23, 37-38, 50, 64, 107, 117, 175-176

Tata Energy Research Institute 134

Tehsildar 3, 99

Territorial Army 81

Transportation 52, 84, 141

U

United Nations Development Program 128

United Nations viii, xiii, 21, 41, 47, 112, 128, 167

Uttar Pradesh iii, v, 5-6, 8, 17, 23-24, 39, 50, 76, 78, 84, 88, 108, 110-111, 117, 119, 123-124, 127-128, 132, 150-151, 176-177

Uttarkashi 33, 84, 127, 167

V

Vivekanand Kendra 107

Volcanic Activity 15

W

Water and Dams 63

Waterways 56, 68

West Bengal v-6, 17, 23-24, 37, 45, 54, 57, 72, 108, 110, 117, 119, 122, 124, 150, 177

Willy Willies 35

World Bank 128, 152

World Disasters Report 15-16, 22, 49, 67, 89, 103, 163

Biographical Information

Prakash Singh has served at the highest levels of law enforcement in India's most turbulent areas–Nagaland, Assam, Punjab, Kashmir, and Uttar Pradesh. The Government of India, in recognition of his contribution to national security, awarded him "Padma Shree," one of the highest awards given to a civil servant. Among his numerous leadership positions, he served as Director General of the Border Security Force, Director General of Police, Uttar Pradesh, and Director General of Police Assam. In these positions he gained a first-hand appreciation of disaster management operations.

Mr. Singh holds a Master of Arts degree in History from the University of Allahabad, and served as Assistant Professor, Department of History at that University for a brief period before joining the Police Service. He continues to lecture at Indian colleges and training academies and in international fora on topics related to terrorism and transnational dangers. His publications include: *Nagaland* (National Book Trust, India), *The Naxalite Movement in India* (Rupa & Co., New Delhi), and numerous articles in Indian newspapers and international journals. He serves on the editorial board of the International Association of Counterterrorist and Security Professionals, and the international journal, *Low Intensity Conflict and Law Enforcement* (UK).

Dr. Graham H. Turbiville, Jr. is Director of the Foreign Military Studies Office (FMSO), Fort Leavenworth, Kansas. Dr. Turbiville's work has appeared in numerous journals and books. He is the editor of *The Voroshilov Lectures: Materials From the Soviet General Staff Academy*, a multivolume series addressing a range of strategic, operational, and tactical issues. Dr. Turbiville's current areas of research and publication include transnational threats, Latin America security issues, and issues of Mexico-United States relations. He is the editor of the international journal *Low Intensity Conflict and Law Enforcement*.

William W. Mendel is senior analyst with the Foreign Military Studies Office. He served as a tenured faculty member at the U.S. Army War College where he held the Maxwell D. Taylor Chair of the Profession of Arms. He is coauthor of *Campaign Planning and the Drug War,* Strategic Studies Institute (SSI), 1991; *Interagency Cooperation: A Regional Model for Overseas Operations*, National Defense University Press, 1995; *The CINCs' Strategies*, SSI, 1997; and *Strategic Planning and the Drug Threat*, SSI, 1997. He has published numerous journal articles on government and security issues.

www.ingramcontent.com/pod-product-compliance
Lightning Source LLC
Chambersburg PA
CBHW070912270326
41927CB00011B/2547